SUCCESSFUL
FREE-LANCING

CONTENTS

1.   THE FREE-LANCER'S GAME   1

Getting at the Heart of Free-lancing • Pros and Cons of Free-lancing • Reasons to Free-lance • Are You the Type to Free-lance?

2.   GETTING STARTED   13

Choosing a Business • Analyzing Potential Clients • Choosing a Legal Structure • Money Talk • If You Lack the Funds to Free-lance • Getting Started

Acknowledgments

Although I have free-lanced for many years, I could not have written this book without the help of other free-lancers, who shared their experiences and information with me in most generous ways. I am especially indebted to the following people, who also gave generously of their time: Sharon Kapnick, Bryan Johnson, Barbara Zimmerman, Nicol Knappen, and Deborah Drier.

Special thanks go to Shelley Martin, a partner at Weikart Tax Associates, who read the tax chapter for accuracy and also offered many excellent suggestions.

And finally, special thanks go to Judy Waggoner for her editorial suggestions and for typing the manuscript. As always, her editorial eye proved invaluable.

Foreword

Within the last several years, the ranks of the free-lancer have swelled massively in numbers and in diversity. The self-sufficient life-style of the independent entrepreneur is a way whose time has come. There are three reasons for the expansion of free-lancing. First, larger companies, in an attempt to reduce overhead, have farmed out many operations formerly executed by in-house staff. Independent professionals in advertising, sales, writing, design, graphics services, and many other areas have benefited from this tilt toward outside expertise.

The second major reason for the upsurge in free-lancing stems from the astonishing development of unusual services. My own specialty of organizer did not exist ten years ago; neither did the profession of the wardrobe analyst, the "surrogate wife," and many other one-person service enterprises. My guess is that these services will continue to expand, especially in professions that lift some household burdens from the harassed two-career family.

And third, the increasingly footloose and free tone of our society encourages people with distinctive skills to set off on their own. People can make their way across the country—or throughout the world for that matter—as independent computer programmers, word processors, tutors, translators, and dog groomers.

With this growth in numbers and diversity comes the recognition that free-lancing is a serious business with potential for earning substantial income. In order to realize that potential, while enjoying the freedom that was probably the impetus to go independent in the first place, what does the free-lancer need to know? The chief requirements are: how to identify prospective clients; how to market oneself; how to make proposals or presentations; how to clinch sales; how to negotiate fees; how to handle contractual arrangements and legal responsibilities; and how to run an office and find extra help when needed. And perhaps most important, one must be able to coolly assess the traits of temperament and personality that are necessary for a successful free-lance life.

Until now, each free-lancer has had to work out the answers for these questions by trial and error, reinventing the wheel so to speak, because there was no body of knowledge or communal experience upon which to draw. Marian Faux's book *Successful Free-lancing* fills that gap in two ways: by addressing the issues raised above, and many others, thoroughly and with clarity, and by forging out of the strands of experience of many individual practitioners the sense that the free-lancer's option is indeed a viable career choice, and that the free-lancer, though independent, is not alone. This book is a welcome addition to the library of anyone who is—or is thinking of becoming—a free-lancer.

STEPHANIE WINSTON
Author, *Getting Organized: The
Easy Way to Put Your Life in Order*

Introduction

Although the number of workers who are self-employed increased by more than 20 percent during the 1970s, and is expected to increase even more in the 1980s, few people think of free-lancing as a full-time, permanent career. People tend to free-lance when they are between jobs, when they want a break from full-time work, or when they are in the midst of making a new career choice. Most persons who free-lance have somehow been pushed into it, either because they have been fired or because their companies have relocated or revamped to the point that they find themselves unemployed. While these people admit that they enjoy their free-lance lives, they also readily acknowledge they would never have planned to free-lance; it is something people fall into because of mostly unexpected circumstances. Even those who have free-lanced for a number of years often leap at the chance to take permanent, full-time work when the right offer comes their way.

It is no wonder, either, that so many free-lancers give up so easily. Few free-lancers are able to rave about their success or even to count themselves as prosperous as their counterparts, the small-business owners. Free-lancing can be—and for too many is—a hand-to-mouth operation, rife with stress and frustration. An argument could even be made that some free-lancers prefer life this way. They seem to think that stress and frustration over money are the prices they have to pay for their freedom, which they rarely have time to enjoy because they are always too busy scrambling to survive financially.

Unfortunately, this is a view that is perpetuated by the nonfree-lancing world. As one free-lancer noted, "I think lots of the people I work for would like to do what I do. The grass is always greener on the other side of the fence. But since they aren't brave enough—or whatever it takes to free-lance—they appease themselves by thinking that I am really poor, that it is almost impossible to survive financially as a free-lancer. Free-lancers aren't supposed to be successful. That goes against their romantic image. Unfortunately, it is easy to buy this line of thinking."

Most free-lancers lament that they love everything about the life except the financial insecurity. But are all free-lancers financially insecure? Is free-lancing a constant struggle? Is financial insecurity the price you have to pay for a life that is otherwise so attractive? Not necessarily. Some free-lancers do quite well. A free-lance business consultant earns $80,000 a year telling companies how to operate more efficiently. A free-lance costume designer earns a minimum of $20,000 each year and sometimes soars into a much higher income bracket. A free-lance magazine writer earns between $50,000 and $60,000 annually. He says he could earn more if he wanted to work harder, which he doesn't, because by his standards that is about what he needs to live well. A free-lance decorator earns $30,000 a year and still has time to donate to the historical preservation projects she loves.

What do these "success" stories have in common? What do they know that so many free-lancers do not know? The answer is painfully simple: All these free-lancers think of their work as a business. All these free-lancers run their professional lives in a highly organized, businesslike way.

But many free-lancers would be quick to point out that they are not motivated by purely financial rewards. Many people free-lance because it gives them the freedom to pursue other, and to them, more serious work. One painter who had struggled for ten years said, "I will not even touch work that might distract me from my art. Earning very much money would distract me." But only a rare writer or artist feels this way. Most readily acknowledge that their lives would be far easier without money worries. Everyone—even those who have no drive to get rich—works better and feels more creative when precious energy is not wasted worrying about paying the rent.

And worrying about paying the rent is not something that any free-lancer should have to worry about. Anyone with the inclination and interest can learn to run a business-oriented free-lance career—and still have time left over to pursue serious work. This book is all about how to do this. It is about the free-lance business as opposed to the free-lance career. Anyone can have a free-lance career. You have one from the day you plug in an answering machine and start taking in free-lance work. You wait, and people call. You do the work as it comes along, often taking in projects that do not pay enough to offer any measure of financial security. You sit around and chew your nails to the quick when there isn't any work. That's what too many free-lance careers are all about.

A free-lance business, on the other hand, entails investigation and planning even before you start working. It involves finding exactly the right area in which to free-lance. It involves taking the initiative to round up clients; it involves soliciting new business before you need it.

In this book, you will learn how to run your free-lance career like the business it is. You will also learn how to make that career a permanent, full-time business, one that will thrive in good times and survive the bad ones. Such topics as setting up an office, deciding on and laying in office supplies, setting up and maintaining a records system, planning for and soliciting new business, servicing old clients, creating your own benefits package, figuring out when to subcontract, and planning a secure future are covered. You will learn how to minimize cash-flow binds and how to extricate yourself from the rare one that is unavoidable. You will learn how to organize your day so that you operate at peak efficiency. You will learn that you do not have to be a workaholic merely to survive the free-lance rat race—that you should and can have time for yourself, clothes, vacations on a regular basis, and money in a savings account.

Anyone who works as a free-lancer—by definition, anyone who provides services, as opposed to products—can improve his or her chances of survival in the free-lance business. Although this book has been carefully honed to the needs of those who run small service businesses, it also contains many ideas that will be of interest to the proprietor of a small business and to self-employed people who make and market products rather than services.

In the 1980s, the number of self-employed persons will grow. The economy is expected to remain erratic throughout most of the decade, which means that companies will offer little security and employees will feel little loyalty. In such times, workers conclude, quite correctly, that they can do as well, if not better, by working for themselves.

An unsteady economy also breeds a rapidly shifting job market. Free-lancers are in high demand to handle the tasks left undone by workers who have been laid off. Many signs point to the fact that free-lancing could be the best career option of the next decade for millions of people. It will also be an increasingly competitive career choice as the numbers of free-lancers continue to swell.

Anyone who is planning to free-lance or to continue free-lancing in the coming years, needs to know about the *business* of free-lancing. No free-lancer can afford to ignore the commercial aspects of this career choice. This book is written to help new and experienced free-lancers run a successful free-lance business.

The Free-lancer's Game

1

Some gurus of the job market predict that the Corporate Age is on the wane and the Age of the Self-Employed Person is coming on strong. Over 8 million people are currently self-employed, either as free-lancers or as small-business owners. This represents an increase of more than 20 percent since 1970, a sudden upturn after more than a century of decline in the number of the self-employed. Demographers are in agreement that the number of free-lancers will continue to rise throughout the 1980s—and probably throughout the 1990s, for that matter.

There are several reasons for this. The trend toward more free-lancers is part of an emerging new pattern in employment. People who used to work at one profession their entire lives, rarely change jobs, and retire at the ripe young age of sixty-five now change careers (often several times), frequently change jobs, and retire later or possibly never. Given these social changes, it is inevitable that more people will turn to free-lancing, either temporarily or permanently, in the next few years.

Retirees often free-lance at second careers. Women who feel they have commitments at home often free-lance. Men and women who have gotten into the corporate rat race and suffered the consequences often find that they want out, and free-lancing offers a way. And the new work ethic that emerged in the 1960s, which decreed that people had a right to expect satisfaction from their work, has been enough to catapult many otherwise ambitious souls into their own free-lance enterprises.

GETTING AT THE HEART OF FREE-LANCING

Lots of people, including many who are contemplating becoming free-lancers, would be hard-pressed to give an accurate response when asked to describe what a free-lancer does. Among those—mostly free-lancers—who understand, there is still a tug on the ego when others persistently refuse to acknowledge the kind of work free-lancers do. One woman, a free-lance photographer's representative for several years, half wailed, "A lot of the time, I think people on the outside have no idea what on earth free-lancers do. I'm sure my mother hasn't got a clue what I do." Another free-lancer, a writer who spends hours doing research in the New York Public Library and in various university libraries, said, "Whenever I tell someone that I'm currently working in a library, they say 'Oh, did you get a job?'"

For the record, a free-lancer is someone who sells his or her services. Some professions support many free-lancers and traditionally always have—publishing and theater are two of the better examples. Musicians, artists, and writers often free-lance because there is no other way to run their professional lives. Teachers free-lance. So do librarians, fashion designers, photographers, models, public relations people, therapists of all kinds, and many people who work in the media. Consulting is nothing but a fancy word for free-lancing. Even the world's oldest profession is a form of free-lancing.

Free-lancers do not sell products, or if they do, it is because they define their services as products. This is what sets free-lancers apart from small-business owners, the other group of persons who are always lumped, along with free-lancers, among the self-employed. Apart from this obvious difference, though, there is reason to believe that some psychological differences separate small-business owners from free-lancers. Small-business owners are often people who are seeking to attain the American dream of owning and operating their own businesses, who believe in Horatio Alger and success and ambition. Free-lancers, on the other hand, are more likely to be driven by the opposite impulse: dreams of freedom and independence. They do not want to create pint-sized domains similar to the ones where they have worked all their lives; they want to get away from the organized and highly structured world of business. Barbara Zimmerman, who has carved out a comfortable niche for herself as publishing's only free-lance copyright editor, subscribes to this idea, "I think there is a difference between people who free-lance and people who run small businesses, even though running a small business is a high form of free-lancing. It would be interesting to know why someone chooses one over another. I think free-lancers want their freedom, and that governs a lot of what they do."

A free-lance set designer talked about the issue of independence, saying: "I watched my father run a small business. He had employees, he worried about payroll, and he bought turkeys for people at holiday time. He was his own boss in one sense, yet his time was not his own. He had obligations. I hate the thought that I might someday have to hire a secretary or an assistant. I like my independence, my smallness. I may have responsibilities, but I have few obligations. I'd like to keep it that way."

Lots of free-lancers are independent souls. They were not especially rebellious when they worked for someone else, and few had personality problems with bosses or co-workers, but most simply never felt comfortable in offices. Stephanie

Winston, a free-lance professional organizer, recalled those feelings, "The real reason I left my job was that I don't accept authority easily. I don't like other people telling me what to do. Some people who don't deal easily with authority get rebellious, but I didn't do that. I got withdrawn. A boss can be the most benevolent authority in the world, and I still don't like his authority. I realized that as soon as I took my first job out of college. I didn't know how I would get out, but I knew I would—so that's why I knew I would grab the chance to free-lance."

Barbara Lee, an especially soft-spoken photographer's representative, shared similar feelings: "I fell into free-lancing when I knew I couldn't stand working for anyone else again. The man I worked for fired me right after I returned from a vacation because he couldn't afford me. He said he could hire someone cheaper than me to do the paperwork. Then, the following spring, he called me and said, 'Well, are you ready to come to work again? Are you ready for another season?' I probably would not have taken the plunge if I had not been fired.

"I had been fired a couple of times. This was not the first time. I kept thinking, 'I'm a nice, conservative, upstate New York girl. Why is it that I'm getting fired?' The reason was that I resented the bureaucracy. I resented the paperwork. I found it difficult to work with people stupider than myself. I'm not usually abrasive, or at least not when I'm comfortable. But put me in a position where I'm up against the wall, and I do rebel. On Monday morning, when I have to appear someplace, I'm up against the wall. It was a ridiculous way to live."

To return to the subject of how free-lancers differ from small-business owners, free-lance operations are usually smaller. Even rich, successful free-lancers run operations that are smaller than small businesses in terms of their simplicity, if not in terms of money. This fact, though, should not keep a free-lancer—present or prospective—from running his or her free-lance career like a small business. Successful free-lancers recognize that one has to be part financial expert, part office manager, part supply clerk, and even part therapist to oneself to make a free-lance operation successful. Many free-lancers simply do not know how to run a free-lance career like a business, using accounting, management, and sales techniques that are valuable in other businesses. But the suggestions in this book are offered with full appreciation of the fact that free-lancing is and always will be a simpler operation than most other businesses, and that most free-lancers have chosen this lot in life because they are independent spirits.

PROS AND CONS OF FREE-LANCING

Anyone thinking about a free-lance career in any area has to consider the advantages and disadvantages. Here are some advantages:

- If you run your free-lance career like a business, you have better than a fifty-fifty chance of achieving financial success.

- You will have the freedom and independence to plan your own work and organize your own time.

- You will have an enormous sense of fulfillment, personally and professionally.

- You will enjoy freedom from control by others. There is no boss to tell you what to do and when to start; no company policy to establish your vacations or holidays.

- You will own your work. A newspaper reporter who went to work as press aide for a senator quickly realized that he was turning out a huge amount of written material and getting credit for none of it. "Since much of it was fiction anyway," he joked, "I decided I might as well write some fiction on my own. So I began my life as a free-lance writer."

- You can work out of your home, which means you have no commuting costs, and you can be around to supervise children if necessary. This advantage is mixed, admittedly, since time spent supervising children is time away from work. Several free-lancers worked at home and still hired outside help to attend to their children's needs during work hours.

- You can work in two or more fields at once.

- You can work odd hours if that is your style.

- There is, in theory at least, no limit to the amount of money you can earn. What you earn will depend upon your time, talent, and commitment.

There is relative simplicity in free-lancing. Even though this book offers many suggestions for ways to organize and manage your free-lance career, they are made with an eye toward preserving simplicity, keeping the business dealings with which you must contend to a bare minimum so that you can do your real work.

There are some disadvantages, too:

- The hours are long, especially when you start. Although they will taper off as you become more successful and charge more for your services, many free-lancers report that they must undertake periods of heavy work. There is no one to share the work with.

- There is paperwork and recordkeeping in any kind of free-lance business. When you start, you have to put together and maintain your own benefits package, something your boss probably did for you. You have to maintain financial records for the IRS. And you probably have to maintain a set of records related to your clients.

- Free-lancers spend many hours, sometimes days, alone. Even those free-lancers, such as artists' and advertisers' representatives, who spend many hours each week calling on people to obtain work say the contact they have with people does not compare with the camaraderie of daily office work—and many report that this kind of social contact is more frustrating than none at all.

- It may be hard to regulate your cash flow—a particularly stressful problem. No one pays you every two weeks or once a month, and often free-lancers are owed a lot of money at the very time they are struggling to figure out how to pay the rent.

- The responsibility is sizable—there is no one to pass the buck to. If something goes wrong, *you* fouled it up. That is more responsibility than some people want to cope with. In addition, you must take responsibility for all the benefits your former employer supplied.

- The security can be less than on a full-time job, although this point is debatable. Barbara Zimmerman, for example, recalls how she started free-lancing because she thought it offered more security: "The company I worked for was sold. They tossed a coin to see who would get fired. They fired an outstanding executive who was fifty-five and had four kids in college. I said to myself: 'That's always a possibility.' I thought to myself, 'Why not freelance—now?'"

  On the statistical side, in 1978 a presidential panel found that only 25 percent of retired persons collected any money from employee pension funds. Of full-time workers in private industry, only 34 percent were even partially vested in employee retirement funds in 1979. Given what a free-lancer who is the slightest bit astute can do to take care of himself financially, there is obviously room for debate over whether a full-time job for someone else is more or less secure than free-lance work.

REASONS TO FREE-LANCE

Apart from the advantages and disadvantages, there are many legitimate reasons that might drive you to give free-lancing a try:

You dislike the restrictive atmosphere in an office.
Your present work is boring.
You are independent.
You lack job advancement opportunities in your field.
You are unemployed.
You want postretirement work.
You want to earn more money.
You won't be promoted anymore in your present job.
You welcome a chance to test your entrepreneurial abilities and creativity.
You want a chance to love your work.

ARE YOU THE TYPE TO FREE-LANCE?

To free-lance, you need three things: skills, background, and the right personality. Before setting out to free-lance, you should do some serious self-analysis to make sure you have the right combination of these traits to be successful.

Skills and Background—How to Get Them

Except in rare fields where you can apprentice as you free-lance, you must acquire the necessary skills and background before you start. For most people, this means years rather than months of working for someone else. You need the benefit of the evaluation you receive from others more experienced than you and of a work setting where you can learn from your mistakes without paying a personal—often financial—price.

In addition to specific work skills and background, a certain amount of sales and managerial ability is needed. Many free-lancers lack business experience; if you are one of these people, take a few courses in management and business before you strike out on your own. You might also think about the

following questions to see if you have indeed developed the
skills and background you need to free-lance:

- Do you know why you want to free-lance?

- Have you worked in an area where you hope to free-lance
  for at least five years and preferably longer?

- Have you acquired any new skills you need to free-lance?

- Are you willing to work long hours? Weekends?

- Have you had any business training, or will you get some
  before you start free-lancing?

- If you will eventually hire employees, have you ever worked
  as a manager?

Do You Have a Free-lancer's Personality?

Certain personal traits are also needed to free-lance successfully. You need lots of self-confidence, plus an ability to
withstand rejection. You need good negotiating skills. One
free-lance editor-writer thought the ability to tolerate isolation
was one of the more important traits a free-lancer needed:
"You not only have to be able to work alone, but you have to
be able to discipline yourself when no one is looking over your
shoulder. The rest of the world generally thinks you have
much more freedom than you have. Friends will call you just
to chat. They will expect you to be free in the afternoon when
they are in from out of town or simply need to talk to someone
about their career problems. A free-lancer has to say no to
most of these requests, just as he would if he worked full-time
in an office."

Free-lance librarian Bryan Johnson said, "You need an
ability to organize your time, but at the same time, an ability
to stay flexible. Also, the ability to take pressure is important.
Free-lancers can bite off more than they can handle. You can
have four jobs due on Friday, and here it is Wednesday

already." Barbara Lee pointed out another trait that most free-lancers need: "I have an ability to say no. That helps in free-lancing. One of my photographers wanted me to work out of his office. I said absolutely not. I knew he worked fourteen hours a day, and I couldn't. My end of the business did not require that. I figured he didn't need to see me on a slow or nonproductive day. Most important, though, I simply know how to say no."

Free-lance editor Sharon Neely thought an ability to tolerate money pressures was important, as did many free-lancers. Neely reported: "I think the money is the biggest thing. There are times when money doesn't come in because you haven't done anything. Those times are rare, though, if you are diligent about pursuing work. But then, there are times when you have done a lot of work and people owe you thousands of dollars, but they aren't paying you. It can make for sleepless nights, and you'll get an ulcer if you don't learn to handle that kind of pressure."

Although only you can decide if you have the personal traits you need to succeed at free-lancing, the following quiz may provide some things to think about:

1. _____ Do you like other people? Even if you work alone, you still have to sell yourself, and to do that, you must like others.

2. _____ Do you welcome responsibility? You had better, since you are the chief, the only chief, in your business.

3. _____ Are you a leader? Leadership may not sound like a trait required of someone who works alone, but it is imperative. It is what will make you a self-starter.

4. _____ Do you make decisions easily? You will have lots to make, so you had better be decisive.

5. _____ Are you a hard worker? This is a necessity, possibly for a long stretch of time.

6. _____ Are you highly organized? Again, this is a necessary ingredient for success.

7. _____ Are you a self-starter? Free-lancers do not sleep late, take two-and-a-half-hour lunches, or go to the movies every afternoon at four o'clock. They force themselves to stay inside and work even when they want to be somewhere else.

8. _____ Are you disciplined? Can you set and keep regular hours? Will you miss your boss prodding you to make deadlines?

9. _____ Are you outgoing enough to sell yourself?

10. _____ Are you healthy? Stamina counts for a lot when you free-lance since there is no paid sick leave.

11. _____ Are you resourceful? Will you know what to do when you hit a slump? For that matter, will you know what to do when more work than you can handle comes pouring in?

12. _____ Can you live with insecurity?

13. _____ Can you live without praise or much reassurance from superiors? Almost no one calls a free-lancer to say that a job was well done.

14. _____ Can you stand constant pressure to find work?

15. _____ Are you willing to forego promotions and raises as signs that you have done a good job?

If you cannot answer at least ten of these questions with a yes, then free-lancing is probably not the job for you, regardless of how badly you want to do it.

If you believe that your skills, background, and personality are those of a successful free-lancer, then the next step is to write a summary of yourself, describing your strengths and weaknesses in the areas just discussed—discipline, organization, initiative, and so on. Do your personal traits match the specific kind of work you hope to do? Are your skills enough to sell you? Can you do the work once you have gotten the job? If you have any doubts about your ability in any of these areas, you should hold off before you start free-lancing.

AWED, a federally funded, nonprofit organization that provides free management and technical assistance, offers these hints to anyone who is thinking about free-lancing:

- Know your market.

- Do not leave a well-paying or an otherwise good job unless you have the money to do so. Usually, that means six months' worth of savings or work that you can count on.

- Appraise your talents fairly before you strike out on your own.

- Be prepared to do paperwork; it goes with the job.

- Know your business cold.

- Be prepared to sacrifice.

- Set your fees as high as possible when you start. (More on that in chapter 5, "Setting Fees.")

Almost everyone knows a successful free-lancer who is not all that good at the technical or artistic end of his or her work, someone who does not necessarily provide first-rate services, but who nonetheless manages to survive fairly well. What makes it possible for these people? A gimmick? There is no gimmick involved, no secret ingredient. Free-lancing has a lot to do with having the right skills, background, and personal traits, but beyond that, you also need to be aggressive, well connected, in the right place at the right time (not as much a matter of luck as of diligence), and very business-oriented.

Getting
Started

2

Free-lancing becomes a serious business proposition when you actually start to make plans about how to set up and run a free-lance operation, once you have decided that you do indeed have the personal traits, the financial wherewithal, and the background and skills. Setting up a free-lance operation involves deciding what area you want to free-lance in (and have a reasonable chance to be successful in), choosing a legal structure, making budget plans to accommodate your new career, and setting goals to get started.

Most new free-lancers make the mistake of not thinking in businesslike terms soon enough. Old free-lance hands, most of whom only gradually became interested in the business aspects of free-lancing, say this puts you at a disadvantage. One reported, "My advice to anyone starting out is to treat the whole thing as a serious business rather than as a carefree venture. Until you realize you are running a business, you cannot be successful." Another commented: "Too many free-lancers who are starting out subscribe to the saying that hand-to-mouth beats nine-to-five, which is another way of saying that free-lancers expect to be poor because they are going to have all that independence and freedom. Well, let me tell you, free-lancers do not have all that much freedom and independence, especially in the first year or so when you really have to hustle to establish yourself. We work very hard, and we should expect to be paid for our work. But you have to approach your free-lance career as a business if you are going to obtain much success."

A businesslike approach should begin before you start to free-lance; preferably, when you have just begun to consider what kind of free-lance operation might be right for you.

CHOOSING A BUSINESS

The first step, strange as it may seem, is to choose the business in which you will free-lance—to match yourself to a business that will offer some opportunity for success. Because free-lancers sell their services, most would-be free-lancers think the area they will free-lance in is perfectly obvious. They will do what they have been doing, only on a free-lance basis. But this does not always work, for numerous reasons, and it is dangerous to make the assumption without first doing some thinking and investigating. Your skills and background may not be strong enough for you to free-lance in one area. You may lack the contacts, or the competition may be too stiff for someone at your level of expertise. There may not be any need for free-lancers in the field in which you hope to work. One woman investigated the possibility of setting up her home as a child-care center. Her teaching credentials were impeccable, and she had enough space in her home to set up a playroom. She lived, however, in an isolated neighborhood, eight miles out of town, and when she finally took a quick poll of the families in her immediate neighborhood with small children she was forced to admit that the opportunities were limited. Of those families with children, most mothers did not work and thus had no need for her services. Reluctantly, she recognized that there was little market for her free-lance services in her present community.

Persons who work in publishing, where there are many free-lancers, often plunge head-first into a free-lance operation doing basically what they have been doing for someone else. Editors become editors, managing editors become copy editors, and so on. Jane Jones, a New York–based editor with a ten-year track record, decided to do exactly this. For the past four years, she had worked as a senior editor and had spent most of her time not working with manuscripts but working with authors and buying manuscripts. She was in a dead-end job—the market was tight, and her chances of moving up were not great—and she wanted some more time to herself than she was getting in her current high-pressure job. Copy-editing, something she had done only for about three years when she was just starting out, seemed the logical choice. She thought of herself as an editor. Jane took the plunge with no fore-thought and no planning.

After about six months of copy-editing manuscripts, she had to conclude that all was not well professionally. After giving the situation some thought and talking to many colleagues, Jane realized that she missed being a manager. She liked the wheeling and dealing of her old job, and there was none of that in her free-lance work. Furthermore, she lacked the precision and attention to detail that made a really good copy editor. What she knew, her clients were undoubtedly learning. Her heart was not in her work, and her skills were less than they should be. To add to her woes, her money was running short. She had not calculated what she would need to live on monthly, nor had she looked into what she was likely to earn in her first year as a free-lance editor.

Belatedly, Jane embarked on a serious search for the right free-lance career in publishing. Using her network, she soon found herself sitting in the office of a book packager—someone who finds a writer and a publisher, puts them together, and then takes responsibility for delivering the finished book to the publisher so the sales force can sell it. She found packaging appealing: she could use her managerial skills; she could wheel and deal again. She believed—correctly, it turned out—that she knew enough writers and enough about production to work as a packager. An added bonus was that she would be expected to come up with book ideas, something she had particularly enjoyed when working as a senior editor. Within three months, Jane had put together two book packages and had several more in the works. She was looking forward to a prosperous career. Had she investigated all this prior to leaving her job, she would have not wasted most of her first year of free-lancing trying to find the career she was best suited to pursue.

Free-lance careers are easiest to find in fields where free-lancing is accepted—publishing, theater, consulting, teaching. It is more difficult to embark on a career in an untapped area. Stephanie Winston did just that. At the time she started her business as a professional organizer, no one else was doing what she proposed to do. Her instincts told her there was a need for such a person, and she correctly sensed that her timing was right. Confident that her services would not only be accepted but also would be in demand, she moved on to the problem of how to let people know that such a person as a professional organizer existed. Based on her success, Winston believes that would-be free-lancers should investigate new, untried areas. She notes, "There is a tremendous, wide-open market for individual services that did not exist ten or fifteen years ago. For example, there was no such thing as a personal organizer when I began. There was no such thing as a personal shopper or wardrobe consultant. I think there are tremendous opportunities—especially since there are so many women working. For example, in my book I mentioned a woman who hired a taxi to take her kids on their afterschool round of activities. Now you have to be wealthy to afford that, but what about some service to do that—a jitney, maybe? There are tremendous numbers of services that can be identified and could support a free-lancer."

While looking around for the right business, there are a few things you can do to make your investigation more systematic:

- Decide what you hope to do, and base your initial research on that. If possible, pick two or three areas in which you might develop a free-lance career. They can be in entirely separate fields or, more likely, they will all be related in some way to the field in which you now work.

- Talk to others who do what you hope to do. Find out how lucrative their work is, how hard they have to work, how long it took them to get on their feet, how much they can expect to earn.

- Also test your idea on people who would be potential customers and on any friends who have good business sense in general. Barbara Lee found that talking to someone outside her field not only gave her a fresh perspective but also provided a steady source of advice after she started her business. She said, "One thing I've found unbelievably helpful is a good friend who has a business of his own but is not in the photography business and who knows nothing about it. He's completely naïve. But I often turn to him for business advice because he has such a remarkably fresh attitude about it."

- Get figures from trade associations, the chamber of commerce, city development associations, and any other groups in your community that help those starting new businesses. If you are a woman returning to the workforce, check to see if there is a local group especially designed to help you get started. Minority people may find there are special groups attuned to their needs, as will retired people planning to free-lance in a new career. Definitely pay a visit to a government printing office and, if one is accessible, the regional office of the Small Business Administration. Both are invaluable sources of information.

Evaluate the information you have gathered. If possible, draw up a list of pros and cons, using the point system. The higher the score, the greater the disadvantage. For example, the fact that competition is tough may not bother you if you have many years of experience and many contacts, so you might assign that a value of 5 on a scale of 1 to 10. The fact that the area in which you hope to free-lance is in a heavy state of flux because of rapidly changing technology might be worth 10 points, especially if you could not afford to invest in the new equipment.

Finally, try to estimate the possible profit—what you can expect to earn when you start out and what you can possibly earn if you are successful. If the cons outweigh the pros, begin the search again and see if you cannot find another area that offers you a better opportunity for a free-lance venture. Remember that the business you choose must be a good match with your skills and background and also with your personality traits. If it does not match on all counts, you are likely to be unhappy or unsuccessful or both.

ANALYZING POTENTIAL CLIENTS

The value of analyzing potential clients cannot be over-emphasized. You may want very badly to free-lance in a certain area, and you may even think that you have come up with a new area in which to free-lance. That is wonderful if you have. There are many successful free-lancers who dared to take that step into something untried. But if there are no clients for your services, then you do not have a business, and no matter how new or how solid your chosen career area is, without analyzing who your clients are and how they will need and use your services, you only increase your chances of failure.

Draw up a potential client profile, in writing, that defines (1) who your potential customers are; (2) whether they will need your services on a regular enough basis to support you; (3) who your competitors are; and (4) whether they are few enough so that you will have a chance at success.

Pinpoint exactly who is likely to want and use your services, how often they will use them, and what they are likely to pay for them. In analyzing the competition, consider whether or not the area is saturated with people offering services that are the same as or similar to what you hope to offer. Do other free-lancers in your area seem prosperous enough, or do they struggle along at subsistence level? Did many go out of business last year? Were there valid reasons such as a recession, or is this the going failure rate? In other words, why does the competition fail? Consider what your successful competitors charge. Can you reach the same market easily and with reasonable expense? Can you make your rates competitive with theirs and still earn what you need to live on and run your business?

Finally, who or what will be your major competition? Remember that free-lancing is essentially a small-time operation, so if you will be competing against a large business or corporation, you must consider carefully whether or not you can hold your own.

CHOOSING A LEGAL STRUCTURE

Once you have chosen the area in which to free-lance, the next step is to decide on the legal structure that will be most advantageous to you. Although most free-lancers work alone, some do choose to have partners. Nancy Mazer and P. J. Fuller, two enterprising women who joined forces several years ago, are an excellent example of a free-lance partnership that works. Their business is also unusual in that it breaks one of the cardinal rules of free-lancing, which is that you should, as much as possible, narrow down the area or areas in which you offer services. Mazer and Fuller provide a range of services, from typing to helping people settle into a new city to finding an unusual birthday gift for someone. They have been successful. Part of their success is undoubtedly due to the fact that they were smart enough to team up with one another, an act that gave them more validity as a business than either would have had alone. As a solo act, either woman might have lacked the credibility because of the scattershot approach to the services they offer; together, they make it all work as a business.

Although partnerships are rather rare among free-lancers, incorporation is not. If you think you might need or want a partner or that you might incorporate, here are some things to consider:

- Why do you need a partner? For the money? Experience? Moral support? All these are valid reasons, but you should be clear about which one(s) apply to you before you start a partnership. The reason for forming a partnership should be a subject of open discussion between you and any potential partners.

- What are the pros and cons of going it alone versus forming a partnership, or for that matter, a corporation? It is not enough to admit that you are too scared to go it alone since that still may be the best course of action for you. Before you form a partnership or corporation, think about the advantages and disadvantages; there will always be some of both.

- Have you discussed your needs with a lawyer? This will help you analyze the financial advantages and disadvantages, particularly where the issue of incorporation is involved.

- What do others in your field do? If few people form partnerships or are incorporated, there is probably a reason, and that is usually because there are too few financial advantages. If many people are incorporated, you can bet that there is a reason for that, too.

Kinds of Legal Structures

The kinds of legal structures available to free-lancers are:

Sole proprietorship—a business owned and operated by one person.
Partnership—two or more persons acting as co-owners.
Corporation—as defined by Supreme Court Justice Marshall in 1819, this is "an artificial being, invisible, intangible,

and existing only in contemplation of law." In laymen's terms, it is a method of business organization that is distinct from the person or persons who own it.

Free-lancers often establish something called a private corporation; it is designed to suit the needs of one person who wants the advantages of a corporate structure. Musicians, physicians, lawyers, writers, and sales people are among those who use this legal structure to advantage.

There are advantages and disadvantages to each legal structure that have to be considered carefully.

Advantages and Disadvantages of Sole Proprietorship

The advantages of a sole proprietorship are its ease of formation, the fact that you own all the profits, and that you control the decision-making process and answer to no one but yourself. A sole proprietorship is the most flexible form of legal structure and also the form that is most free of government control and taxation.

The disadvantages are the fact that you and you alone are liable for any debts. You are also liable personally, that is, your house and other belongings can be taken in any claims made against you. Less money will be available to you in the form of bank loans and lines of credit. Especially in the case of free-lancers, there is the double liability of being a sole proprietor and a free-lancer who sells services and thus has no inventory to use as collateral when seeking capital. Long-term financing is almost impossible to obtain. Your business often cannot be handed down in a family or sold if you die or want to get out. Sole proprietorships often end with the death of the owner, and free-lance sole proprietorships do almost without exception. If you have a family, this may be a major consideration.

Advantages and Disadvantages of a Partnership

There are many kinds of partnerships, and if you are thinking of forming one, you should consult with a lawyer who can explain the possible arrangements to you. The differences among the various kinds of legal structures are also well explained in the Small Business Administration (SBA) pamphlet, "Selecting the Legal Structure for Your Firm," available free by writing SBA, P.O. Box 15434, Fort Worth, Texas 76119. Most free-lancers seek active partners, that is, persons who will be full participants in the business, but some find partners who offer financial support and little else.

The advantages of a partnership are that it is easily formed and relatively free of government regulation and special taxation. It offers much the same flexibility of a sole proprietorship. As in the case of Mazer and Fuller, two persons acting together are often stronger than two persons acting individually, and a partnership offers such advantages as shared management and twice as much experience and skill as a sole proprietor would have. In certain cases, a partnership can obtain financing more easily than can a sole proprietorship.

The major disadvantage is that you must share your profits and your interest in the business. If your partner is active, you must take his views and management ideas into account. Furthermore, in a partnership, at least one partner must have unlimited liability such as a sole proprietor has. A partnership is unstable in that it is dissolved if one partner leaves the partnership or dies, although you can buy partnership insurance to cover this possibility. There also may be difficulties if one partner wants to buy the other one out; a way to avoid this is to write arrangements for executing this into the partnership contract. Finally, one partner acting as agent can make decisions that are binding on the business.

Advantages and Disadvantages of Incorporation

The advantages of a corporation are the limitation of liability (your personal possessions cannot be taken in payment of debts), simplicity of transferring ownership, stability, and ease in securing financial backing. Aside from limitation of liability, though, none of those advantages are likely to apply to a free-lancer. A corporation does not ensure stability or any better shot at financial backing than you might have otherwise; you cannot transfer ownership of a business that sells services very easily, and you are only as secure as the amount of business you hustle.

Apart from that, there are some real advantages to free-lancers, albeit qualified ones, thinking of forming a corporation. The tax rate may be lower. You can write off more insurance. Your health insurance, for example, might be part of the benefits package you receive from the corporation, and until the 1982 tax law took effect, you could set up a corporate retirement plan with an annual limit of $36,875 as compared to $7,500 or 15 percent of your income for a Keogh (whichever is smaller), the retirement plan that free-lancers most often establish. The annual limit for Keoghs is now $15,000 or 15 percent (whichever is smaller), and it will probably continue to rise in the future, thus making incorporation a less enticing option.

The disadvantages are that you must cope with many government regulations and reports to be filed on the local, state, and federal levels and that you are double-taxed—you must pay personal income tax and corporate income tax. The expense of forming a corporation is also high, ranging from $1,500 to $5,000, depending upon where you live. (Sometimes, you can do most of the work of incorporating yourself and cut the costs to about $500).

Whether or not you incorporate depends upon your financial status. Most experts say you should be earning between $25,000 to $100,000 before you think about incorporation. The range is so wide because cash flow is also an important consideration. To take advantage of the higher retirement investment rate, for example, you must have the cash to invest. If you make $125,000 but need $100,000 to live on, then the benefits of a private corporation are probably not great enough for you.

If you incorporate, you also cannot income-average (see chapter 5, "The IRS and Free-lancers"), something that many free-lancers find themselves able to do because their income fluctuates so drastically from year to year.

Setting Up Your Legal Structure

Whatever legal structure you decide to establish, at some point you should have your plan looked over by a lawyer or possibly an accountant or financial planner. Before executing your legal structure, ask an expert to check or draw up the contract required. You should also check with a lawyer when you are involved in litigation, have credit problems (people are not paying you), and when you are preparing to subcontract or hire people to work for you.

MONEY TALK

The next major issue confronting a would-be free-lancer is money, and it is a big one. Taking the time now to plan your finances and review your financial needs means you will have more security later.

Four considerations are important when you start to think about the money you will need to start free-lancing:

1. Do you know how much money you will need to start the business and to live on while you start it?

2. Do you have the money to start?

3. Can you borrow money or get credit?

4. Are you willing to take a temporary cut in pay?

Personal Expenses

The best place to start is with your personal expenses, which must be met every month. Also, you will probably use your own cash to support your free-lance venture for a few months anyway. Thus, you need to figure out how much money you have and how much is needed to meet your monthly expenses. If need be, keep a running record over several months to get an accurate estimate of what you spend. Fill in the charts on pages 25–26 to determine this. The extra space at the bottom of the charts is for any categories you might wish to add.

INCOME

	Monthly	*Annually*
Savings account		
Pension (Will you get anything when you leave your present employer?)		
Dividends, interest (from stocks, money funds, etc.)		
Gifts and bonuses or vacation pay to which you may be entitled when you resign		
Unemployment (if you are eligible)		
Wages from job assignments or part-time job		

ESTIMATED MONTHLY LIVING EXPENSES
(personal)

	First Month	Second Month	Third Month
Housing (rent or mortgage)			
Utilities			
Phone			

Food
  At home
  In restaurants			

Insurance
  Homeowner's and renter's
  Medical, which you must
  now pay in entirety			

Medical and dental			
Loan repayments or debts			
Savings account (Yes, you should still maintain one)			

Special savings fund (for
    purchases such as home
    upkeep and furniture,
    clothes)			

Transportation			
Entertainment			
Vacations			
Child care			
Miscellaneous expenses			
Inflation factor (add 10 percent)			
TOTAL PROJECTED EXPENSES			

Estimate your expenses in each category. Then examine them carefully. Is there anything you can cut back? For example, you will no longer have to eat lunch out every day, nor will you have to maintain a wardrobe for work if you have a home office. Your commuting expenses will be far less. Can you go without a vacation for a year or two? Be realistic about what you can or cannot live without. Everyone has a personal limit for sacrifice, and you will only be miserable if you do not recognize yours.

Business Expenses

The next step is to project your business expenses. When you are starting a free-lance business, your projected expenses will fall into two categories: start-up costs and operational costs. The former occur only once, and the latter are expenses that must be met month after month as you free-lance.

The chart on page 29 lists one-time start-up costs and helps you plan how to meet these expenses. Start by including every possible cost you might have to meet and every possible furnishing you might want to buy. Later, you can go back and revise this chart, based on what you actually will be able to spend. At that point, set up a list of future purchases you would like to make as you become more prosperous and secure.

Now you must add your start-up costs and your estimated monthly living and business expenses for at least the first few months to see if you have enough money to start the free-lance business. These expenses vary so much, depending upon the kind of business you are starting and such things as whether or not you will maintain a home office, that there is no accurate way to determine how much money any one free-lancer might need. To be on the safe side, though, regardless of what kind of free-lance business you are starting, you should try to have an amount equal to what you will need to live on and to run the business on for six months.

There are exceptions, of course. If you resign your full-time job but still have a trust or income from dividends that will

START-UP COSTS FOR FREE-LANCERS

Item	If you plan to pay cash in full, enter the full amount below and in the last column	If you are going to pay by installments, fill out the columns below. Enter in the last column your down payment plus at least one installment.			Estimate of the cash you need for furniture, fixtures, and equipment
		Price	Down payment	Amount of each installment	
Furniture	$	$	$	$	$
Equipment:					
typewriter					
phone machine					
tape recorder					
radio or television					
other					
Office supplies *					
Decorating and remodeling					
Utilities deposits					
Legal and accounting fees for setup					
Insurance *					
Professional fees and dues *					
Advertising and marketing for setup					
Operating capital					
Cash to live on while business gets going					
TOTALS	$	$	$	$	$

*These are ongoing expenses, but they must be included in set-up costs because you will need money to finance them initially.

ESTIMATED MONTHLY BUSINESS EXPENSES

Item	Estimated Cost
Your salary (what you need to live on per month)	
Salaries and wages of persons whom you subcontract to work for you	
Rent for office	
Advertising	
Phone answering service	
Other utilities	
Messenger and other services	
Office supplies	
Other professional supplies	
Insurance	
Taxes and social security	
Legal and accounting fees	
Transportation	
Entertainment	
Professional memberships	
Repayment of loans	
Miscellaneous	
TOTAL	

allow you to support yourself, you have few worries. More realistically, if you have already landed a huge free-lance job that begins the day after you put the finishing touches on your office and that runs for six months to a year, then you can reduce the amount of back-up capital you will need. Even so, you should still try to have three to four months' worth of money to live on at all times. Eventually that job will run out or you may hit a dry spell, and you must be prepared for this. Every free-lancer needs a sizable emergency expenses fund to cover such periods—or even to use while job hunting if free-lancing turns out not to suit you.

The calculations you have just done are important in terms of helping you decide whether or not you can afford to free-lance at this time. You can always start on a shoestring, but there is one disadvantage in doing that. In a business where most operations are started on very little, if you reduce the amount still more, you may never catch up. You run the risk of always living hand-to-mouth.

IF YOU LACK THE FUNDS TO FREE-LANCE

There are solutions if you do not have the money to set up a free-lance business. The most obvious is to stay on your job until you have saved enough money. Another is to obtain as much credit as possible before you start free-lancing. Get a line of credit now while you are employed; get major credit cards. Solicit a loan from a friend or relative who believes in you—just be sure to include regular repayment in your estimated monthly expenses. Solicit business projects before you start to free-lance, or moonlight as a free-lancer until you have saved enough money to feel secure free-lancing full-time.

GETTING STARTED

Once you have determined that you have the funds to free-lance, the next step is to begin to establish operations. The remaining chapters are devoted to such things as setting up your office, arranging your finances, dealing with the IRS, and getting and keeping clients.

Setting Up an Office

3

Setting up your own office can be the most exhilarating part of starting your own free-lance business. It is the time when you begin to see some tangible proof that everything you have been carefully planning is actually going to happen. And one of the nicer things about setting up a free-lance office is that you can often do it cheaply. The investment in your office can be as small or as large as you want—or need—it to be. Fortunately, how much you spend has little to do with the kind of environment you ultimately create for yourself. One enterprising free-lancer created a broad work surface using wooden sawhorses, with doors as table- and desktops. Her file cabinets fit neatly under the doors, and she bought several old bookcases secondhand and painted them bright blue.

If you will call on your clients, you certainly can get away with investing very little in fixing up an office. On the other hand, if your clients will be meeting with you at your office, you may have to spend a bit more, but again, the amount you spend has little to do with the result if you're willing to do most of the labor yourself and look for secondhand office furniture.

PLANNING THE KIND OF OFFICE YOU NEED

Before you jump into planning an office, consider your needs very carefully. To start with, do you really need an office? If you are a consultant who will be working mostly in other people's offices, you may be able to get along, as one free-lance wardrobe planner does, with a file cabinet in your linen closet and a shelf or two devoted to office supplies. On the other hand, if you are an artist, you will need considerably more space in which to work, although it probably will not be an office per se. Of more importance to you than where you can store supplies, for example, will be the kind of light you need to work by. Editors and people who work in publishing also require a lot of table space in which to spread out their projects and reference materials. Sooner or later most free-lancers need an office, however, if only some kind of a cubbyhole in which to store a file cabinet.

After deciding that you need an office, the next important question is where to locate it. The answer depends on a combination of your personal and business needs. Judy Waggoner, a free-lance typist and copy editor, is also the mother of four small children. For her, she noted, there was no choice: "I maintain an office at home, because only there can I combine my two roles—mother and editor—most efficiently."

Most free-lancers opt for a home office because they believe it is cheaper than an outside office and because they like the income tax deduction it gives them for their rent or mortgage payments. Some free-lancers do not even consider the alternative to having a home office. Sally Chapralis, who worked as a free-lance public relations person for many years in Chicago, said: "I maintained an office in my home. At that time I assumed it was the only way to handle free-lancing, particularly in the economic sense. I wasn't knowledgeable or sophisticated enough to realize that there were other options. But it worked out well enough."

Others do not so much plan for a home office as they let it emerge and gradually take over a part of their living spaces. This happened to Bryan Johnson, a free-lance librarian: "I bought an IBM Selectric for work. And I got filing cabinets. Then I got a table that is separate from my personal desk. It has no knickknacks—it's just for work. Now I've even rearranged my apartment since I've realized how busy I am with the free-lancing. My office is in a corner—near a window—where I can work without distraction."

Pros and Cons of a Home Office

There are decided pros and cons in having an office in your home, just as there are pros and cons to having an office outside your home. Here are some reasons to maintain a home office:

- The aforementioned tax deduction. You can deduct part of the rent or mortgage payment of your apartment or home. One word of caution here: You can deduct only the part of your mortgage that is not interest. If you have just bought a home and most of your monthly payment goes for interest, you may not be able to take a deduction for a home office as well. Since you already write off part of the interest, to deduct a home office on top of that would be a double tax break, something the IRS frowns on.

- There is usually no pressure to decorate, as there might be in an office outside your home.

- There is no commute to and from the office. This saves not only time but also money. You don't have to hassle with the weather, nor do you spend much on lunches, as you might be tempted to do if you worked in a business area or an office where you have others to lunch with.

- Your time is, in some respects, more flexible. You can go to work when you want to and take breaks when you want to. And you can run errands in your neighborhood anytime you wish.

Some of the disadvantages of a home office? Free-lancers report the following problems:

- Working at home can be lonely and stifling. Chuck Wall, an editor who tried free-lancing and found it wasn't to his taste, recalled his free-lance days: "I didn't like working at home at all. I missed the personal contact, and I missed the office hustle and bustle." Even those who plan to continue free-lancing can feel that way—and they are the ones who need an office outside the home. Another free-lancer reported: "I couldn't create at home. I had quit my job in anticipation of this highly creative life in my own space—*my* home office. After two weeks, I returned to my former employer, who was going to be my main client anyway, and asked for office space, which he gladly rented to me for a nominal fee. Now, seven years later, I still free-lance, and I still have my cubbyhole in my ex-employer's office. He's still a client, but I also have lots of other clients."

- You can waste a lot of time—valuable time—procrastinating in your home office. The sight of a dirty room, the temptation of a new book, a sudden urge to have home-made split pea soup for lunch all can become major distractions when you work at home.

- Finally, some free-lancers report that they hustle less when they have only one ·rent to pay. One book indexer commented: "Let's face it, I know I can earn less money because I have my office in my home. I earn enough every month to pay the rent and my other bills and to give myself spending money. I'm thinking about sharing an office with someone else or several people who work in publishing. It would get me going—in more ways than one. But the first thing is I would have to earn that extra rent."

Pros and Cons of an Office Outside
Your Home

But there are also reasons to decide on an office outside your home. A big one is the need for company while you work. One woman, who had been earning her living as a free-lance magazine writer for over ten years, started with an office at home and moved to an outside office as quickly as possible, an unusual move for a writer, since they usually thrive on the solitude. She reported: "I tried working at home and quickly realized I simply could not handle it, or at least it did not feel right to me. It was a struggle to get out of bed, and even more of a struggle to get to work. I felt even worse than when I was struggling to get up and go to someone's office to a job I didn't particularly like. I explained my problem to a friend who worked for a publisher, and she helped me arrange to take space in her boss's office. That's where I've been ever since. It has worked out really well. Left to my own devices, I am something of a slow starter, and I don't get to the office much before ten. But once there, I'm a hard worker, and I rarely leave before six or seven. I'm usually the last one to leave—which is something of an office joke since I'm my own boss."

To many free-lancers, an outside office feels more professional, especially if they have to meet with clients. If you plan to receive many clients an office not only may work best outside your home or in a separate room, but it often has to be fancier than most home offices. An outside office also separates your professional and personal life in a way that a home office does not. For free-lancers who tend to be workaholics, this can be another plus.

On the other hand, there are disadvantages in having an office outside your home:

- It costs more because you must pay a separate rent as well as separate utilities.

- You have some added expenses in setting up. At home you can work in a chair in the living room or at the dining room table if you must for a few weeks or months, but an office outside your home won't be of much use to you until it is set up with a desk, telephone, and other office appurtenances that are necessary for you to conduct business.

- You will also have to spend money on lunch and commuting.

- You will probably need to dress up more than you would if you were at home, especially if your office is in a business section of the community where you live.

- You will find that your work schedule is more rigid than when you work at home. The urge to work may well come over you at 11:00 P.M., but you won't be likely to get dressed and trek down to the office at that hour. Most free-lancers who maintain offices outside their homes report that they tend to work fairly regular hours—nine to five—while free-lancers who work at home tend to work those hours and then some.

YOUR OFFICE LOCATION: A PERSONAL DECISION

Ultimately, where your office is located becomes a personal as well as financial decision. Barbara Zimmerman advocates a home office for free-lancers despite its disadvantages: "When you move out of a home office, you move into rent, electric bills, a business phone, clothes, and you lose all the tax advantages of having an office at home. It's a large chunk of money to have an office outside your home. Also, I work irregular hours. And I have a very busy season in the summer. I often work until 1:00 A.M., and I wouldn't do that in an office. I have a compulsion to get things done. I don't know whether it's good or bad, but it means that I need an office in my home."

On the other hand, Robyn Cones, a free-lance masseuse, has had it both ways and feels more comfortable with an office outside her home, even though she now works at home so she can care for her small child. She thought it helped her business, too: "It's better outside—for my clients, that is. Coming to a masseuse makes a person vulnerable. You come and take off all your clothes, and if it is in someone else's home, it makes you that much more vulnerable. If it is an office—however homelike it is—the client can make the place his own. I think my office should not be sterile. I like it to have lots of wood and plants, for example, but I also think it is good for my clients to know that no one lives there. Now that I work in my bedroom, it's harder. But there is a corridor for clients to walk down, and once the stereo is on, they will, I hope, feel as if they are in a special place. I'm also having a Murphy bed built, so my clients don't look at my bed or feel as much as if they're in a bedroom."

Another woman, a free-lance artist's representative who now works in an office in her home, thinks of getting out: "I do eventually want an office outside my home. I now store my portfolios, which weigh about forty pounds, at a small art studio near where I make calls. Eventually, I will probably be able to rent a space from them for about $100 a month. I will definitely do it as soon as I can afford it. This is too hard, working at home. I can see my office reflected in a mirror from my bed. I hate that."

What it all boils down to is that free-lancers, depending upon their personalities, decide whether they want to work in or out of their homes. For those who do not want to work at home, even the benefit of a tax deduction does not carry much weight. And for those without much money who cannot stand to live and work in the same place, there are always deals to be negotiated, space to be traded off for business favors, ways to band together with others in a similar situation. The important thing to remember is that you can always try one thing, and if that doesn't work, then you can do something else. Once you have decided where your office will be, the next step is to set it up.

What to Look for in an Outside Office

If you want an office outside your home, the first step is to locate an adequate space for it. Before looking for office space, consider the following:

- How much space do you need to work in? Will a tiny corner do, or do you need a studio space? What kind of storage space do you require?

- How fancy must your office be? Will you be the only person seeing it? Will clients come to your office? If so, will they drop by for a few minutes, or will you need to have lengthy meetings there with them?

- What, if any, special features, do you need? Must the lighting be natural or artificial? Do you need a sink? Lots of electrical outlets? Any special temperature? Special ventilation? Make a list of all these special needs before you look at office spaces.

- What kind of location do you need? Do you want to be close to your home? To your clients? Do you need access to a messenger service?

What to Look for in a Home Office

When you start sizing up your home for a corner or room that would make a nice office, keep these things in mind:

- Will there be enough storage space or enough room so you can build in what you need?

- Will the office be accessible to the services you need, such as copying, typing, messengers?

Finally, consider whether or not the place where you hope to have your office is zoned for business. This is no problem in apartments in large cities such as Chicago and New York, but in the suburbs and in small towns, you may live in a residential area where businesses are not permitted. If this is the case, and your neighbors are touchy on this point, they probably will only tell you after you have established an office. If, like most free-lancers, you will keep your office low-key and you will not advertise in any overt way, there may be no problems. However, if you have frequent deliveries or must have a sign or some other form of advertising, then you may run afoul of zoning regulations. Or you may have trouble just because your neighbors don't like the idea of a business in a residential neighborhood.

To find out whether or not your prospective office site is zoned for business, contact the local zoning office. Or better yet, pay them a visit. That way, while you're there, you can check to see if any noisy or otherwise obtrusive construction is planned during the time you hope to stay in the office.

Leases and Office Space

If you plan to have your office in your home, no adjustments need be made to your lease, although if you are looking for an apartment and know you may start free-lancing during the term of the lease, it may be best not to announce your business plans to any prospective landlords. In Manhattan and Chicago more than one free-lancer has found the rent taking a sudden jump when the landlord discovered that the apartment was also to be used as a place of business.

Once you've signed a lease, this is no problem, and you can quietly begin your free-lance operation. Of course, if you already free-lance full-time and are getting a new apartment, then your landlord will have to be told what you do for a living. Play it down, if possible, so you don't invite an increase in rent.

Before you sign a lease for an office outside your home, there are a few things you need to know. Commercial rent is usually based on square feet of space. Business leases tend to run longer than domestic leases, but often there are no set rules about the length of the lease. This is frequently a negotiable point—to your advantage. For example, if you want a six-month lease, you might be able to get it for office space, or you might be able to get a five-year lease. Be sure that the lease runs for a period of time that suits you—whether it is only for a few months or a few years. And if possible get an option to renew for several years. Landlords will often do reconstruction to suit your needs in a commercial space. If you need such provisions, be sure the lease specifies *in writing* what remodeling or reconstruction work that is to be done. If you are going to do the work yourself, this fact also should be mentioned in the lease.

FURNISHING AN OFFICE

The special needs and supplies of artists and craftpersons and others who need studio space are too diverse to describe here, and besides, those people know what their special requirements are. What the following pages do describe in detail are the supplies and office equipment you need to set up an efficient business office.

When you think about shopping for furniture for your office, you must consider whether you want—or can afford—to decorate or whether your office will be makeshift at first. There is nothing wrong with a makeshift office put together over several months or even years. In fact, this is often the best kind because such an office will emerge as a highly usable workspace suited exactly to your personal needs. One book that can help you with ideas as you get started on an office is *Worksteads: Living and Working in the Same Place* by Jeremy Joan Hewes (New York: Dolphin, 1981).

If you do not have a lot of money to spend, consider buying secondhand furniture. One free-lance writer based in Manhattan haunted the secondhand office furniture shops near Canal Street and ended up with an office reminiscent of the early 1940s. He found some old wooden file cabinets that were inexpensive yet very well built. You could not buy cabinets so well built in most furniture stores today. His large partner's desk (no, he doesn't have a partner, but he occasionally works as a free-lance editor and claims he uses a different side of the desk for each activity) would cost thousands of dollars if he tried to buy either a new or an antique version in good condition; he got it for $350 and restored it himself. Secondhand office furniture stores specialize in perfectly usable, modern secondhand furniture, but they also frequently have items that are both funky and cheap as well as old, period furniture. Don't expect to find top-of-the-line, very expensive, or custom-made furniture in this market. You can buy furniture in good condition, and if you are willing to refinish and paint yourself, you can get some genuine bargains.

The next level up in office furniture is, economically speaking, contract, or office, furniture. Office furniture is often very well built and is, for some reason, less expensive in many instances than furniture designed for home use. Probably one of the more expensive ways to furnish your office is to buy department-store furniture designed for home use. Elaborate copies of antique furniture and pretty flowered or printed upholstered sofas in your office will not be inexpensive. The most expensive office furnishings you can buy are genuine, high-quality antiques. One young psychiatrist, who was making a lifetime investment in his office and wanted it to be impressive as well as comfortable, bought an 1860 accountant's desk with a tooled-leather top for about $2,000.

Finally, don't forget you can rent office furniture on a short- or long-term basis. Furniture rental is usually inexpensive, and if you aren't willing to buy a lot of furniture before you are sure your business will take off, this is an excellent way to furnish an office. A four-month rental on a large L-shaped desk in a large city runs about $180; smaller desks go for about $140, or about $35 a month. A secretary's chair rents for about $10 a month; a five-drawer file rents for about $18 a month. A standard desk and chair cost about $38 per month. Get several estimates before you rent anything; prices not only vary from community to community, but they vary from store to store.

If you are really pinching pennies, see what you already have on hand that might be used to set up an office. Or consider building simple office furniture. You can even sell yourself furniture you already own to furnish your office, especially if you are incorporated. Just remember to declare the money you earn as income on your personal income tax form.

The list below will help you with your initial planning. Put a check beside the items you must have to start off; put an X beside the items you would eventually like to own but can do without right now. On the blank provided on the right, write down possible places where you might obtain each item.

SHOPPING LIST FOR OFFICE FURNITURE

_____ desk_____

_____ chair_____

_____ wastebasket_____

_____ file cabinet(s)_____

_____ extra chair(s)_____

_____ in and out baskets_____

_____ bookshelves and other storage_____

_____ ashtrays_____

_____ coffeepot or teapot and cups_____

_____ any other dishes you need; kitchen supplies_____

_____ clock_____

_____ bulletin board_____

_____ sofa_____

_____ table_____

_____ radio_____

_____ fan or air conditioner_____

_____ lamps_____

_____ art to hang on walls_____

_____ pencil and pen holder_____

EQUIPPING AN OFFICE

Once you have decided on basic furniture, the next major purchases you have to consider are the office machines you will need, such as a typewriter, adding machine, small calculator, or even a computer. You may find that when you start out it makes more sense to buy office equipment than to invest in furniture. Based on the 1982 tax reforms, you can write off the first $5,000 of equipment you buy without depreciating it at all. This amount is scheduled to increase to $10,000 by 1986.

If you can't afford new equipment, consider investing in used equipment. It will even earn you a tax credit (see chapter 5). A rebuilt office model typewriter, depending on its age, can be purchased for $450 to $700 or $800. Many writers and editors invest in reconditioned office typewriters, particularly C and D models made by IBM. These machines are about fifteen to twenty years old and they can be expected to provide another ten years of service—even the kind of heavy-duty service they get from professional writers. Prices vary, depending upon where you live, so be sure to shop around. When buying a reconditioned typewriter, be sure to buy from a dealer who comes highly recommended—preferably someone your colleagues and friends have been satisfied with. Other office equipment can also be purchased secondhand. Check the Yellow Pages for the listings on the specific piece of equipment you need.

Occasionally, you will find a dealer who will sell many kinds of office equipment, but often, equipment dealers are specialists. The person who sells you a typewriter will not be able to sell you an adding machine. For items such as hand-held calculators and radios, find a good discount appliance store and buy from them. Postage machines, should you decide you need one (most free-lance businesses are too small for this), can be purchased from special dealers also listed in the Yellow Pages.

Do You Need a Computer or Word Processor?

Finally, you may want to consider whether or not you need a small, personal computer or word processor. You're probably blanching at the thought that you might need such a machine or wondering how you could possibly use one even if you did own it. But even if this is your view, you should still look into buying—you might be surprised at how you could put it to use and at how much time and money it can save you. Major manufacturers such as Apple, Wang, Xerox and IBM are moving into the personal computer market, and several suppliers such as Apple and Radio Shack have made their names in supplying personal computers for home use that are well suited to the small business and independent entrepreneur.

The purpose of computers is to process information—and everyone from a schoolchild to a housewife does that. You will certainly do that in your business, which is why you may in fact be an ideal candidate for a personal computer. On the other hand, the kind of computer that is needed to help in a small business or the kind of word processor an editor or writer requires can cost thousands of dollars. The minimum invest-ment for a personal computer that you can use in business is around $2,000, and it can run as high as $10,000, depending upon the kind of software and storage capacity you need. Then, too, computer technology is changing in such a way that the prices will probably be reduced in the next few years, as will the physical size of computers. If you cannot afford to invest in one now, it is still something to keep in mind for the future. An hour or so spent talking with a computer sales representative will be worth your time for future reference.

If you cannot afford to invest in a computer now but could still use one, there are two possibilities: time-sharing and using a service bureau. When you work with a service bureau, you hire them to process data and produce reports and other materials you require. Such services run anywhere from $300 to $1,000 per month for a small business. In time-sharing, you rent the terminal device that connects you to a data-processing center. This method is faster and cheaper than using a service bureau; the monthly rental of the terminal is about $150 and the hourly charge typically runs about $10. Information is turned around more quickly (within minutes) when you use the time-sharing method, whereas a service bureau may require several days a week to process your information and get the material back to you.

Setting Up the Phones

While a computer is likely to be the kind of equipment you can invest in only after several years of free-lancing, a telephone is a necessity for every free-lancer, as is a phone answering machine or an answering service.

In most states, the rates for business phones are considerably higher than the rates for nonbusiness phones. Few free-lancers have reason to announce to the phone company that they are using their phones for business. If you do, you may only end up paying a higher rate for a business phone.

If your office is in your home, you are strongly advised to have another, separate, line put in. There is something about knowing that a free-lancer works at home that makes people feel they can call at all hours of the day and night. Your best protection against this is to have one phone that is used exclusively for business. The second phone is your private line. Just make sure that you never give your private, or home, number to any prospective client.

Often, a free-lancer who is starting out is eager to take any and all business calls. This quickly wears thin, however, particularly when clients call during dinner or late at night. Of course, you can always have a private line put in further along the line, that is, after you have established yourself, but it is more professional to have your business phone separate from your private phone when you start free-lancing. How you arrange this depends on the services the phone company offers where you live. In Chicago, for example, it is fairly inexpensive to rent a phone with push-button lines; in Manhattan the same system runs several hundred dollars for installation, and the monthly rental rate is considerably higher than the personal rate. Alternately, in areas where a multibutton phone is prohibitively expensive, you can purchase such services as call waiting or have two separate lines put in if you need more than one business phone.

Finally, consider buying your own phones. For several years now, it has been legal to own your own phones rather than rent them from the phone company. Since phone companies often charge a monthly rental fee for the machines you use, you can cut your phone bill by as much as 30 percent per year by owning your own telephones. You can cut costs even further by buying a reconditioned, basic black telephone. Check your local Yellow Pages for listings of stores that sell telephones and telephone equipment.

There is one disadvantage to installing your own telephones, and that is the phone company will not provide free service to repair a broken phone that they do not own. On the other hand, telephones are built to last (you can expect to use a reconditioned phone for twenty years or more), and they rarely need service.

In addition to the basic phone lines, most free-lancers need someone—or something—to take calls when they are out or too busy to deal with the phone. The cheapest ways to handle this are an answering service or a phone machine.

Answering services are listed in the Yellow Pages. They offer a range of services, varying from twenty-four-hour pickup to nine-to-five pickup; they also provide varying degrees of courtesy to your callers, and you should not only check out their level of courtesy before you buy their services but also ask friends and clients from time to time how they are treated to be sure that the level of courtesy continues. Answering services charge a monthly fee ranging from $15 to $100; courtesy, unfortunately, is often one of the things you pay for.

An answering machine that can be hooked up to your phone involves a one-time charge for the purchase of the machine and possibly a charge for installation or hookup by the telephone company. Ironically, a phone machine is often viewed as more impersonal than an answering service even if the service is surly. From your point of view, though, a phone machine is less expensive to use over the long run, and it doesn't eavesdrop or know anything about your personal life, which many people consider advantages over an answering service.

Phone machines have become increasingly sophisticated in the past few years. Some have remote control so you can get your messages from anywhere in the world; on some, you can even change your message by remote control. On many machines, you can prepare more than one message and control the number of times the phone rings; on most, you can monitor your calls, which is valuable on busy days when you don't really have time to take every call. If privacy and long uninterrupted hours of working will be important to you, buy a machine that can be turned down so you do not hear the calls when you do not want to. (You can also have your telephone adjusted so it does not ring out loud.)

Shop around before buying a phone machine; prices and levels of sophistication vary. Phone machines are now available in discount appliance stores, where you can spend as little as $70 to $80 for a fairly unsophisticated model to several hundred dollars for a model with all sorts of extras. Good brand names to look for include Panasonic, Code-a-phone, Sanyo, Phone Mate, Record-a-Call, and ITT.

The final thing you should consider if you make a lot of long-distance phone calls for business is one of the private long-distance telephone companies. They can cut your long-distance bill by as much as 40 percent. These companies are advertised on television and radio, and are listed in the Yellow Pages. Not all companies are set up so you can call all areas of the United States, so be sure you will be able to reach the areas you call most frequently before you sign anything.

Other Office Services

Aside from your telephone, part of setting up your office involves locating other services you will need such as copying and printing, messengers, cleaning, and coffee or vending services. Make sure these suppliers are easily accessible to you, and if you have an opportunity to shop around, try to find the cheapest possible source. Although a cleaning service may sound extravagant, many free-lancers, especially those who work at home, hire someone to clean their offices. It is deductible; it is relatively inexpensive; and it is something most free-lancers, who already spend long hours in their offices, simply do not want to bother with. If your office is outside your home, you may have no choice but to hire a cleaning service (the building probably has one), unless you want to invest in a vacuum cleaner just for your office.

Replacing Equipment

One of the smaller joys of starting small or decorating on a shoestring is that you can upgrade as you get richer. And if you don't get richer suddenly or as soon as you had hoped, then you can still upgrade bit by bit without breaking your budget.

Most of the time, you will know exactly what you want to buy for your office and where to get it. As for equipment, though, knowing when it is worthwhile to upgrade can be another matter. Larger businesses use a complicated mathematical formula to help them decide when to replace equipment. In a simpler business, you need only to figure out whether the new equipment (that computer, for example) will be important enough to justify its cost. To do this, make a cost comparison between the two pieces of equipment. Figure out what each costs to buy and operate and whether or not the new equipment will help you earn more money. Take depreciation of each piece into account. If the new equipment will not bring you more business, then you can ignore this factor when comparing costs. If it will bring you more business, then you should take a projected figure into account.

Usually, there will be a decided advantage to replacing one piece of equipment with another, once you compare the two. One editor, for example, who was also beginning to write books, looked into the possibility of investing in a word processor versus buying an electronic typewriter. He was a specialist in writing textbooks and also had garnered several book contracts for adventure books that would be written very quickly and according to a publisher's format. In other words, he specialized in turning out quantity. With a word processor he calculated that he could do one-third more work over the course of a year. His initial outlay would be large—$9,600 compared to around $3,000 for the typewriter—but he would also save several thousand dollars in typing bills since the word processor would run off corrected copies while he was out for dinner. He decided the investment was worthwhile in the long run after looking carefully at the figures for both pieces of equipment. But then when he began to talk with computer salespersons, he soon realized that prices were about to drop for the kind of computer he wanted. Not only that, but computers with more storage capacity at a lower price would be available in the next few years. He began to see that it made more sense for him to buy an electronic typewriter, which would be fairly easy to resell for a good price in three to four years, and to wait that length of time before buying a word processor.

As a general rule, experts advise that you opt for the piece of equipment that requires the smaller investment and has the shorter life if the operating costs of two pieces of equipment are the same. You should also do this when you know that changes in technology will bring about many advances in a piece of equipment during the next few years. On the other hand, if you believe that a piece of equipment will go up in price or that interest rates on a loan you might take out to buy the equipment will be high, then you would be better off buying now.

For the kinds of office equipment most free-lancers require and the relatively small investment involved, most decisions to replace equipment are made by first comparing costs and then by following instincts. If, however, you are thinking of investing in something that requires a substantial amount of cash and/or the support of a bank loan, then you will need to look more closely at the cost comparison figures in the ways just suggested. "The Equipment Replacement Decision," a booklet available free from the Small Business Administration,

P.O. Box 15434, Fort Worth, Texas 76119, will also help you calculate the necessary figures to make a smart decision.

BUYING OFFICE SUPPLIES

One free-lancer reported: "I knew I was becoming a real businesswoman when I started to avidly read the office supply catalogues that arrived in my mail. I soon discovered that another free-lancer I knew was developing a similar affection for office supplies, and the next thing I knew, one of us would jokingly call the other whenever she had made a 'major' purchase or found some new item for the office. It was all a joke, but it was also a lot of fun."

Free-lancers do indeed find that treating themselves to office supplies can be fun, and why not? They are deductible, and as the free-lancer who just described her burgeoning love of office supplies noted, "On a bad day, it's a lot cheaper than hitting Saks Fifth Avenue." The amounts and kinds of office supplies you need varies with the nature of your business, but the following list will set you up with the basics:

pens
pencils
erasers
typing paper (Buy copy machine paper; it is so cheap you
     can use it for second sheets or scratch writing, and it also
     looks good enough to use for manuscripts and reports.)
typewriter correction paper or fluid
scratch pads
memo pads (or use scratch pads)
paper clips
rubber bands
stapler and staples
scissors
tape (clear tape and mailing tape) and tape dispenser
brown paper for wrapping packages

stamps
envelopes in several sizes
mailing labels
clipboard
Rolodex or other storage file for names, addresses, and
    phone numbers
files
filing supplies
small file boxes for index cards
typewriter ribbons

Calling Cards and Stationery

In addition to basic office supplies, you need to think about creating your image on paper through stationery and business cards. More than one free-lancer reiterated the words of the free-lance editor who said, "Getting started was easy. That's one of the things I loved about free-lancing. I bought an office machine, got some stationery printed, and considered myself in business."

Stationery and cards come in all levels of quantity and prices, ranging from what is called instant printing to engraved printing. Unless you can afford to do so, there is no reason to get very fancy, and in some businesses you can even skip a card. A good rule of thumb is that you need a card if you are frequently asked for one; if no one ever asks to see your card, then you don't need one. One free-lancer who moved her editing services business from Minneapolis to Chicago noted, "I had cards printed when I started in Minneapolis. Then when I moved I was on a tight budget and never got around to having new cards made. I discovered that even though people occasionally asked me for my card, no one was upset when I said I didn't have one. I've never gotten new cards." On the subject of cards and stationery, simple is better than fancy. One free-lance typesetter said, "I got very carried away with my cards when I started out. After all, letters were my business. I made myself an oversized and beautiful card. Then gradually, as I became friends with the people I worked for, one or two admitted that they found my cards inconvenient because they were too large to be taped to a small index card or inserted into a Rolodex file. I tossed out my lovely cards and got myself a plainer, standard-sized card."

The cheapest and most practical way to obtain stationery and cards is to buy them from an instant printer who can set the type and print them for a small amount of money. Instant printers charge from $8 to $35 for several hundred business cards; one hundred sheets of stationery and envelopes with your name, address, and phone number on them cost anywhere from $12 to $40 from an instant printer. They would cost several hundred dollars if you had the same amount engraved or had a fine printer do the same work.

Whatever method you use, you need to start by having type set for your letterhead. Type comes in several faces, or styles, and in many sizes. Printers and engravers will usually set type at a small added cost. Or if you know anyone who works as a typesetter or want to buy the type yourself from someone, then ask that person to do the job for you. Type for a letterhead costs from $10 to $80, depending upon the kind of typesetter you use and the typeface you select. Once the type is set, a paste-up or mechanical must be made. Again, the printer or typesetter you use will probably do this for you. Actually, a paste-up may only be needed if you want to position the type in an unusual way on the page, for example, vertically rather than horizontally. If you do not want anything unusual, you may be able to skip most of the steps just described and simply choose a style of stationery offered by the printer. You should ask to proof your letterhead after the type is set, if possible. If you do not proof it and the stationery does not come out right (something is misspelled or wrong), then the printer will redo your job at no extra cost.

Buy a conservative paper. Papers can also often be purchased for very little from an instant printer. (Paper also comes in many grades and styles, and you can end up spending a great deal for it.) It should be at least 20 weight so as not to appear flimsy. White, buff, gray, manila, and tan are the most acceptable business paper colors; you can never go wrong with white. Make sure the envelopes match in color and quality.

Most free-lancers opt for stationery without a logo, probably because they do not want to go to the expense of having one designed. If you do decide on a logo, and perhaps you can select a stock one offered by your printer, keep it simple. One successful copy editor–typist has a small typewriter on her letterhead. It is simple, it gets her point across, and makes her correspondence—especially invoices—stand out on someone's desk. It is a logo that works. Fancy type and overdesigned logos often do not work, and they only make your letterhead difficult to read.

Once you get your stationery, be careful how you use it, strange as this may sound. Certainly you should type invoices on it, as well as confirming letters and letters of agreement. But resist the urge to write a letter when a phone call will do the job. Editor Chuck Wall explained why he viewed letterheads and fancy cards with some degree of suspicion: "When I see the letterhead, I often think this is someone who is going to nag me. I like to speak to free-lancers face-to-face. People who have letterheads tend to be the people who write you every month and who send you Christmas cards and post cards when they go away on vacation. You dread hearing from them because they nag you by letter during the months when you don't have work. You get letterhead after letterhead from them." The message from Wall and several other people who hire free-lancers is that letterheads are great for invoicing and legitimate business communications. But where the custom of more direct encounters, either in person or by telephone, exists, as it does in publishing and many other areas where free-lancers work, you should follow that custom. You will only appear unnecessarily stiff and formal if you use your letterhead where you could better use a telephone.

Shopping for Office Supplies

Before signing off on the subject of office supplies, here are a few pointers on buying and using them:

- Whenever possible, buy in bulk. Most office supply stores offer a 10 to 15 percent discount for quantity purchases. Often, items will not be displayed in bulk, but don't let this stop you. Ask for a box of typewriter ribbons or a box of pens or whatever you need.

- Buy stamps in bulk because it saves time. You go to the post office less often. Stamps are sold in rolls of a hundred, and for a ridiculously low price of about 5 cents, you can buy a plain plastic container for a roll of stamps. In a stationery store, decorative containers cost $5 to $10.

- Reuse office supplies as much as possible. Envelopes can easily be reused; files can be used over and over. One free-lancer noted: "I'm a shameless reuser of envelopes, and I don't care if I send one client something in an envelope from another client. I figure it's a not-too-subtle way to let one know I have other business. On the other hand, if I'm just starting to work with someone, I usually want to impress them with my neatness and sense of organization, so I make an effort to send materials in a fresh envelope—the first couple of times, anyway."

- If you travel a lot for business, or call on clients, set up a briefcase desk so you aren't always dashing around at the last minute before an appointment looking for the office supplies you need. Stock your briefcase or tote bag with invoices, cards, note pads, pencils and pens, envelopes, stamps, and anything else you need.

- If something saves you time, consider buying it. Time is very valuable to free-lancers, and something that might look like a luxury can actually be a good time-saver. For example, one free-lance editor bought preprinted labels, which came only in a quantity of 500 and cost considerably more than the plain ones she could buy in a stationery store. She thought she was doing this because she hated addressing envelopes, and she joked with friends about having to order 500—a quantity that seemed impossible to use up even over a period of several years. To her surprise, the labels turned out to be real time-savers, and she uses them at the rate of about 150 a year. The initial investment of $20 now seems cheap. Remember that one free-lancer's time- and money-saver might be another's luxury. These decisions are personal, but once you realize that something saves *you* money, make sure you stock it.

OFFICE SECURITY

The final thing you have to worry about as you set up an office is how to protect it. Burglary or fire in your office can be even more devastating than a burglary or fire in your home. You can lose work-in-progress, your file of business contacts and financial records, as well as samples of work.

Taking Inventory

Once your office is settled, you should make an inventory so you will have proof of what you own. An inventory will also help you and your insurance agent decide what kind and how much insurance you need. Your homeowner's or business policy may not cover such things as blank checks, manuscripts, and certain records—the very things that you may consider most important. To make a simple office inventory:

1. List each item, the year it was purchased, its original cost, and its present value.

2. Also list the model number, brand name, dealer's name, and a description of the item. Save and attach receipts.

3. Keep a copy of this inventory in a safe place other than your office (a safe deposit box, for example).

4. Update the inventory regularly, possibly as often as every three or six months while you are still buying major items for your office. At minimum, update it once a year.

Physical Protection

A minimum level of protection involves buying a good lock for the door and locks for the windows. Beyond that, consider either a burglar alarm or a safe—or possibly both. Safes are designed for specific tasks, that is, they are either burglarproof or they are fireproof, so you have to decide which is more important to you. You can, of course, purchase a safe that is both, but it will cost you approximately $1,000—a figure that is out of reach for most free-lancers. A good fireproof safe, fifteen by eighteen by twelve inches in size, costs about $200; a similar-size safe that is burglarproof costs about $350. Before you buy either one, check with your insurance agent to see if there are any specific requirements that you can afford to meet. Locksmiths often point out that insurance companies have rather unreasonable requirements that few small business operators actually can afford to meet, but you should check just the same.

Buy the best safe you can afford. Bolt it to something in the office; very large safes have been carried away by enterprising burglars. Never leave the combination anywhere in the office. Even if you have a safe, never leave checks, credit cards, or cash in it if you can possibly avoid doing so.

A burglar alarm offers a second form of security to an office. The best kind is a silent one that goes to a protection agency or a police station, if you live in a community small enough so that police intercept these calls. Such systems are expensive, however, and you may only be able to afford a local alarm that makes enough noise to scare off a prospective burglar. On-site alarms work best when attached to safes or lock boxes. Before purchasing a burglar system, talk to several professionals to get their estimates of what you need and what it should cost.

Organizing and setting up an office is something most free-lancers approach with a great deal of enthusiasm. Unlike an office that belongs to your employer, your own office—whether it is in your home or outside your home—bears your personal stamp. It can also be organized and set up exactly to your taste and needs, and this is surely one of the better "perks" of free-lancing.

The Finances
of
Free-lancing
4

Free-lancers may be afraid of the tax man, but they are mostly
apathetic about planning their financial lives. This may, in
fact, be a major factor in the high attrition rate for free-
lancers. It certainly appears to be what separates the business-
oriented—and financially successful—free-lancers from the
independent spirits—who are often too poor to enjoy their
independence. The most common failing is not keeping a
good set of records. Without that, a free-lancer has difficulty
measuring success in financial terms, as well as in planning for
the future. Most experts, including those in the Small
Business Administration, believe that poor recordkeeping is
directly related to the high rate of business failures for small
businesses:*

* Small Business Bibliography No. 15, "Recordkeeping Systems—Small Stores and
Service Trade," Small Business Administration.

For the individual just going into business, experience clearly shows that an adequate recordkeeping system helps increase the chances of survival and reduces the probability of early failure. Similarly, for the established business owner, it has been clearly demonstrated that a good recordkeeping system increases the chances of staying in business and of earning large profits.

For the majority of free-lancers, though, recordkeeping is something of a short suit, one that most are not even particularly interested in, as this statement by an advertising copywriter shows: "Today, I'm pretty decent about the whole thing. I do try to stay tuned to these matters. But when I started out, I was rotten. The only thing I did was pay the IRS. Were I to start all over today, I would structure my business differently. I would begin with an accountant who specializes in free-lancers. I would have him set up a records system I could easily follow—and one that didn't take too much time." A weaver concurred: "I know I should have a separate business account. Hell, I should at least have a retirement account— that is something I could do for me. But I resist the whole notion of getting involved with that stuff. I free-lance because I like the feeling of freedom, and I guess I'm afraid I won't feel so free if I have to spend several hours a week filling in record books."

Yet free-lancers who don't keep good records are no more likely to stay in business than are small business owners whose records are inadequate or sloppy. But small business owners get a lot of help from their banks and the SBA in setting up and keeping records; rarely is anyone looking over the shoulder of the free-lancer. You have to do it all yourself. Because of this, the free-lancers who do keep good records often took several years to learn how to do so and to find a system that works for them.

Many, such as free-lance furniture designer Connie Pfander, have been delighted to discover that they really enjoyed that part of their businesses once they developed some financial expertise. Pfander reported, "I always thought I couldn't add two and two and stayed away from numbers. But then, when I was thinking about setting up my free-lance business, I took another free-lance job as office manager for some Soho clothes designers. They called in their accountant and had him show me how to keep the books. I thought I was going to hate that, but to my surprise I really loved it. I did those books very diligently, and in the process I learned a lot that eventually helped me get a loan to finance my own free-lance business." She added, "I know lots of artists and craftspeople who think they shouldn't be bothered with paperwork because they are creative people. But since I've gotten involved in furniture design, I also have met lots of craftspeople who are very good at the financial end of their businesses. I now think that creativity and good financial sense often go hand-in-hand. At least, there's no truth to the image of scatterbrained and disorganized artists. It just doesn't have to be that way."

Another good planner is rights and permissions editor Barbara Zimmerman, who said, "I kept good records right from the beginning because I comprehended immediately that my expenses came off my income taxes, and that I had to keep track of them. I keep daily copies of my expenses. I debit instantly which expenses belong to which client. I keep a minimal sort of books, though.

"My financial planning is, unfortunately, even more minimal, although I'm very interested in learning more about that. I hold off all December money or don't deposit it if it comes in the mail. I am finally starting to learn about insurance policies and money. I have a retirement plan, and I'm trying to figure out how to earn more money on that. My business account is separate from my personal account."

Most free-lancers, though, are neither so antibookkeeping as the weaver nor so astute as the furniture designer or the permissions editor. Most keep few or no accurate records; many do not even know how to go about setting up a records system, since few free-lancers have a business background.

THE IMPORTANCE OF
FREE-LANCE FINANCES

There are several reasons why every free-lancer should have a records system especially attuned to his or her individual operation. The most obvious reason is that such a system helps you survive in business. It is also in your self-interest to understand the financial workings of your life. As a free-lancer you will now be responsible for many of the things that your former employer arranged for you. Health insurance, life insurance, and a pension plan are often part of a benefits package supplied by the employer at little or no expense of time and money to the employees. As a free-lancer you are now your own employee, and you now must handle your own benefits. Finally, free-lancers, even fairly poor ones, occasionally accrue large amounts of money. Just as a small business owner would figure out what to do with that money until he needed to spend it, you, too, need to know how to invest any extra money you have if only short-term.

The finances of free-lancing, fortunately, are not very complex. After reading this chapter, even if you don't think you can develop and set up your own system, there is still no reason why you cannot maintain a system that someone sets up for you. And, of course, if you can afford to do so, there is no reason not to hire financial experts to manage your records and your money for you. In this chapter you will learn enough about financial planning to set up your own simple accounting system or to speak intelligently to an expert when you discuss what you want him to set up for you.

Every free-lancer must be concerned with three areas of financial planning. The first is setting up a basic records system so you can keep track of what you spend and what you earn. The second area is budgeting, necessary so you can tell how you are doing and whether or not you are going to survive. The third area is arranging a benefits package that protects you personally and also protects your business.

THE RECORDKEEPING SYSTEM

A recordkeeping system lets you keep a close check on how you are doing financially—what you are earning, how much you have spent, who owes you money, who has paid you— and whether they have paid you the correct amount. Even if you have an accountant or financial manager, you still need to understand enough about the financial underpinnings of your operation to enable you to talk intelligently with him. You will also need orderly financial records if you plan to obtain any kind of financing for your business, especially a loan from a bank or savings institution. The last reason that you need a records system is the IRS. It is through your business records that you must be able to justify any expenses that you deduct. The IRS has no set requirements for records, except that you must maintain permanent records that can be used to identify income, expenses, and deductions. The burden of proof, should you be audited, is entirely on you. What that means is, no records, no deductions. The minimum amount of time you should keep records is three years, and this should include records showing monies received, canceled checks, and invoices. Copies of tax returns should be kept for six to seven years, according to most accountants.

Every records system should be easy-to-use, up-to-date, and accurate. Fortunately, a free-lancer's records system can be highly personal, even idiosyncratic. One free-lance author keeps her most recent records in several plastic three-ring notebooks. One is labeled *Business* and contains invoices, contracts, letters of agreements, royalty statements, budgets, and other records regarding payments. She records expenses in a notebook she carries with her. A second notebook is labeled *Correspondence* and contains all the letters she writes during the course of one year that are related to business. She has found that the system works well for her since she often has to put her hands on certain pieces of information quickly while she is on the phone. She commented: "I ghostwrite for a woman, so we share royalties. Often when we're discussing business, I need a copy of a royalty statement. With the notebook system, it's always right at my fingertips. And my agent and I frequently need to check something on a contract, so all I do is pull the notebook with the contracts off the shelf. I try to put everything in writing, so I like to keep my letters in one file that is always handy." Another free-lancer described her somewhat unorthodox system, one that nevertheless is ideal for her work as a free-lance editor: "My system is less casual than it used to be, but I still think you would say it's casual. I record what I earn every month in a little five-by-eight notebook. I fill in the date I was paid, and the date I sent the bill and a job description. I don't keep carbons of invoices because I hate making carbons. That's why I settled on the notebook. If someone ever needs a second invoice, then I make a carbon and send it to them. If they lost the first invoice, after all, they don't know what it looks like. Then I save all my receipts so I can take the appropriate deductions."

There are many ways to set up your records, but before doing this you need to know what you have to keep track of. For a free-lancer that is usually fairly simple. You need a checkbook. A separate checkbook is preferred by the IRS and some accountants, but many free-lancers do not bother. A checkbook is a record of how much money you spent during a year, how much is taxable, and how much is deductible, assuming that you wrote checks for some or all of your deductible expenses.

You need some kind of cash receipts record. This can be as simple as a file of copies of invoices marked paid and the date you received the money, or it can be a cash receipts journal or even a plain notebook that you have devised for this purpose.

There are two methods of keeping track of your incoming cash: the accrual and the cash method. You need to use one or the other for your income tax records, and you must be consistent in its use. In the cash method of accounting you record the cash when you receive it and when you spend it. Under the accrual method you account for cash when it is earned rather than when it is received. You account for

CASH DISBURSEMENTS

Date	Item	Place	Purpose	Account	Amount
6/14	Phone			Smyth	$11.80
	Cabs			Smyth	$12.30
6/15	Office supplies				$40.60
	Small office equipment				$10.00
6/16	Cab			Smyth	$6.80
	Bus				$.75
	Lunch w/Don Smyth	Brew-It Pub	Discuss new assignment		$35.70
6/17	Air fare to Boston			ABC	$60.00
	Lunch w/Ned Jones	University Club	Discuss account maintenance	ABC	$18.00
	Taxis in Boston				$15.00
	Drinks w/Jennifer Chesler	Terminal Restaurant	Discussed reassignment of account people on Dinnerstein account	Painter & Chatwin	$15.00
	Dinner	Terminal Restaurant		ABC	$5.80
	Taxis to and from airports			ABC	$35.00
6/18	Transportation to and from library		Research on Dinnerstein account	Painter & Chatwin	$1.50
	Office supplies				$3.30

CASH RECEIPTS

Date	Received from	Purpose	Amount
6/14	Smyth	Retainer Fee	$800.00
6/17	Smyth	Payment for Ruddick, Inc., proposal	$1,200.00
	ABC	Payment for annual report (partial)	$2,000.00

expenses as they are incurred rather than when they are actually paid. The cash method is preferred by almost all free-lancers.

Finally, you need a cash disbursements record in which to record your expenses. This shows what you have spent, all of which is deductible when it is directly related to your business. You can simply save receipts. Too many free-lancers stuff them all in envelopes and sort them out on April 13 before they go to see their accountants on April 14, but this is time consuming. More important, it probably causes you to underestimate your expenses for the year and thus not take deductions as large as you are legitimately entitled to. It is far better to keep a regular record in a notebook you set up or in the kind of bookkeeping guide you can buy.

One free-lance illustrator commented, "My accountant chewed me out last year and said I should write down my expenses every single day. She said I would be surprised at how much I spend. So I started doing it recently, and was I amazed. I spend a lot more on transportation than I ever thought I did. I have always estimated it rather than keeping an accurate record. I deduct movies and admission to museums, but I never remember to save receipts. That costs me a lot more than I had realized." The illustrator is now a convert to frequent regular recordkeeping of cash disbursements, and you should be, too. If you can't face looking at figures every single day, then save the receipts and do them on a weekly basis.

Truly diligent free-lancers carry a small expense book with them and record every expense as they incur it. They then transfer these expenses to a larger record, where they also note such expenses as rent and utility deductions and major purchases. Less diligent free-lancers—which means most of us—put receipts into a record book and sit down weekly or every few days to record the small expenses for which there are no written records. If you keep an accurate engagement book, you can usually reconstruct what you did on any one day fairly easily. Only a highly disorganized free-lancer would stuff receipts in envelopes—or worse, in one envelope—and then waste hours sorting them out at income tax time.

There are many kinds of recordkeeping systems, ranging from complex computer programs to simple "one-book" systems. The latter, records kept in one book, are satisfactory for most free-lancers. The Small Business Administration publishes the booklet "Recordkeeping Systems—Small Store and Trade Service" (available free by writing SBA, P.O. Box 15434, Fort Worth, Texas 76119), which contains descriptions of a variety of recordkeeping systems. Some are simple books that cost under $5; others are small, personalized business services that provide a one-time set-up service.

Be sure to check out the one-book systems at your local stationer or office supply store. Ideal and Dome are two brands favored by many free-lancers. Dome also publishes a book called *Expense Account Diary*, which is excellent for keeping track of your expense records.

As you get more involved with your records system, you may want to expand it, or you may need to expand it as your business grows. Additional files you might consider setting up and incorporating into your accounting system are:

Inventory/Purchasing:
   purchase order file
   supplier file
   receipts file for goods purchased
   stock file (needed only if you have an inventory)

Sales:
   record of sales transactions file

Cash Records:
   bank statement reconciliation file

SETTING UP A BUDGET

Once you have established a records system that suits you and your business, the next step is to draw up a budget. A budget is the basis of a recordkeeping system. It can be prepared for any length of time—one month, a quarter of a year, a half year, or a year, or for that matter, for a longer period of time. Most free-lancers think they do not need to prepare a budget, but they do whether they realize it or not. Every time you start worrying about money—usually in the middle of the night— and then finally sit down and add up what's coming in and what has to go out to pay the bills in the next month or several months, you have, in effect, prepared a budget. You will be much better off preparing budgets on a regular basis and filing them where you can easily find them in those moments of panic, rather than always embarking on the midnight search for pen and paper so you can figure out how you stand financially.

A budget is a planning tool. It helps you set a goal and move toward it. It shows whether or not you are making a profit. If you aren't earning as much net profit after taxes as you would be if you were working for someone else, then you are not successful financially, and you must do some serious planning—and to do that, you need to have a budget to look at.

Of course, there are some extenuating circumstances that cause free-lancers to appear to do less well working for themselves than when they worked for someone else. The first couple of years you build up business may result in lowered earnings. A choreographer, for example, might decide to take a cut in pay to work with a promising but poor ballet company. Some free-lancers find that, given the tax deductions they can take, they can actually live just as well on less money than on money earned working for someone else. You know, though, if the guideline just mentioned applies to you. And there is little point to free-lancing—at least on a permanent, long-term basis—if you cannot do as well or better than you did working for someone else. Planning to alleviate such money problems is one of the ways a budget can help.

Ideally, to do a budget you should know what your income will be, something that free-lancers cannot always easily predict when they first start free-lancing. After a while, however, you will begin to have an idea of what your yearly income will be. But before you know your yearly income, to plan a budget you must project your earnings, based perhaps on what you need to earn. For example, you can estimate that you will need to have three or five jobs monthly at $500 each in order to earn enough to live on. Based on this projection, in the absence of an earnings record, you can draw up a budget.

There are many kinds of budgets, but most free-lancers can get by with a very simple one that shows whether they are operating in the red or the black. What follows is a sample form for a very simple monthly budget. Using this, you can tell whether or not you will be able to meet your monthly expenses.

Calculate the taxes you owe (use tax charts) based on your net income. Subtract the amount of estimated taxes that you owe from the total net income, and you will have the balance. If the figure is positive—and enough for you to live according to the standard you like to maintain—then you are running in the black. If the total is negative or very small, then you need to figure out a way to earn more money.

QUARTER-YEAR MONTHLY BUDGET

	First month	Second month	Third month
Beginning cash balance			
Cash collection			
Cash payments Rent Utilities Operating costs			
Total net income before taxes			
Estimated taxes			
Balance			

Before discussing what you can do if you are not earning enough money, there is one more kind of budget you should draw up—one that shows your actual and projected expenses. This form, on page 70, shows whether you are adhering to the budget you have set up for yourself.

When Your Budget Shows a Deficit

If you do not earn enough to cover your expenses and show some profit, then you have to consider what to do about it. There are four possibilities:

1. You can raise your rates, something that, ironically, free-lancers seem most reluctant to do, although it is the first thing most business owners would think of doing in such a situation, if they possibly could. For information on setting and raising rates, see chapter 7, "All About Fees."

ACTUAL AND BUDGETED EXPENSES

Budget this month	Actual expenses	Variation this month	Budget year to date	Actual year to date

2. You can increase your workload. This is feasible in some fields and not in others. Most editors, for example, cannot learn to edit any faster, and their income is limited by how much they can physically accomplish. On the other hand, you can subcontract, that is, hire someone to work for you and take part of his or her earnings. This works especially well if you can find someone to train who wants to learn your trade. You can also often subcontract with colleagues when they are in slow periods. More information on this appears in chapter 10.

3. You can expand into related kinds of work that pay better or that you can do faster. One editor, for example, learned to do indexing. Fewer people have indexing skills compared to the number who copy-edit, and the hourly rate for indexing is higher than for copy-editing and proofreading. A dancer filled his slow periods by starting a cottage industry making leg warmers in his apartment. He hired other unemployed dancers to work for him. There were always enough people around so that he could meet his contract with a major manufacturer, but the dancers could come and go according to their real career demands.

4. Finally, you can reduce your expectations. While free-lancers can and do earn a healthy living, free-lancing will probably not make you rich. As a general rule, unless rare luck strikes, or you are willing to expand through sub-

contracting or finding new and more lucrative areas in which to work, your income will probably not soar dramatically. On the other hand, it should rise steadily, and it must keep pace with inflation.

RAISING MONEY AS A FREE-LANCER

Many people who run free-lance businesses could be helped by an infusion of capital at certain times. Sometimes you have earned the money you need, but your clients are slow to pay. Unfortunately, banks and other financial institutions look rather askance not only at new businesses but particularly at independent entrepreneurs, that is, free-lancers. For some bankers free-lancers just are not big enough to bother with; others view them as too risky to bother with. Either way, the free-lancer has even more difficulty than the beginning small business owner when it comes to borrowing money to run his or her business. But there are a few things you can do to tide you over financially and to obtain some extra money for those times when your clients are not paying you as quickly as they ought to be.

If you have carefully planned your free-lance career and know in advance that you're going to start free-lancing, then try to make the following arrangements *before* you leave your regular job. It is simply easier that way.

- Apply for a major credit card, particularly one you can use for business expenses. You are more likely to get it if you have a company name to put on the application.

- When you have a major credit card, apply for a line of credit or even a small loan from your bank. As a free-lancer you will probably have to show tax returns to verify your income in order to get a loan, and you won't have those until you have been free-lancing for a year. Even then, you are not likely to show high profits for the first few years. So the best thing to do is to get the line of credit before you start free-lancing—again, when you have a regular income you can wave in front of your banker.

Your Credit Rating as a Free-lancer

Once you have free-lanced for a while, you should have little problem obtaining whatever kind of credit you need, provided your business shows a profit. (But if it doesn't, again, why are you free-lancing?) But in order to obtain credit, your credit rating must be sparkling. This doesn't mean, however, that you have to be the promptest bill payer in town. Free-lancers, like everyone else, get into cash flow binds, and at those times you, like everyone else, will probably slow down on paying your bills. The trick is to slow down on the bills that don't matter or get you into trouble.. This varies from community to community. In some cities you can let the phone and electric bill go—that is, not pay it until you receive the next bill or pay only a few days before the next bill arrives. In other communities the utility companies are the first creditors to remind you that you have not paid as promptly as you might.

As a general rule, once you have figured out which creditors won't try to collect right away, pay off your big bills first and let the little ones slide. Occasionally pay off a bill before it is due. For example, if you have charged an airline ticket on a major credit card, pay it off early. This looks good on your record.

Getting a Line of Credit

With a good credit record, once you have free-lanced for a year or more, you will have little difficulty getting credit. Should you want a loan from a bank or savings institution, be sure to go about it in a businesslike fashion. The first step is to develop a business plan that you can show a banker when you request a loan. According to a Department of Labor publication ("More Than a Dream: Being Your Own Boss," U.S. Department of Labor, Employment, and Training Administration, 1980), your business plan should contain the following items:

1. The nature and location of your business.

2. Why your services are needed, if you are asking for start-up money. If you are asking for credit for another purpose, then you should state specifically what that purpose is. Don't tell a banker you want a loan or line of credit to get you over the rough times when your creditors do not pay you promptly; instead, tell him you need the loan to remodel your office or invest in a major piece of business equipment.

3. Who your market is, or how it will be expanded.

4. Who your competitors are.

5. What your expenses are, if you need start-up capital, or how much money you need for an investment.

6. What your earnings are, after taxes.

7. Monthly estimate of your cash position for one year.

In seeking a loan, don't forget there are other places you can look besides a bank or savings institution. Loan companies, insurance companies, credit unions, and commercial credit or sales finance companies are all possible sources of money. Finally, you can also ask someone to cosign your loan for you if you feel you will not be able to get one on your own to finance your business.

Finally, cultivate your friendly banker a little before you request a loan. This may be easy to do if you live in a small community and know your banker personally. It is more difficult but hardly impossible to do if you live in a city. Don't just walk in one day and ask for a loan. Instead, talk to your banker about the kinds of credit that are available. Drop the fact that you run your own business and mention how well things have been going for you. Ask about business accounts and discuss whether he thinks you need one for your business. It is one of the great ironies of this world that bankers don't like to lend money to people who really need it, so you should sound self-confident and successful. After you have established at least an acquaintance with the banker, then arrange for a meeting to discuss the possibility of obtaining a loan or a line of credit. If you are dealing with a neighborhood bank, don't think this means you can show up for the meeting in cutoffs and a T-shirt. Look at least a little businesslike when you appear for the meeting. Have the papers you think the banker will request with you. Have a neatly typed copy of your business plan with you. If you have cultivated the banker's acquaintance, if you are well-prepared, and if your income and credit rating qualify you, the chances are good that you will get the loan you need.

GETTING HELP FROM EXPERTS

Many free-lancers believe they do not earn enough money to need financial advice, but the Consumer Financial Institute of Massachusetts says that anybody with an after-taxes income of more than $20,000 can use some financial advice. This goes double for someone in business for himself or herself. Many kinds of advisers are available, such as stockbrokers, lawyers, accountants, credit counselors, bankers, and insurance agents. One of the newer services is that provided by a financial planning consultant, a generalist who can help you with overall financial planning.

Before hiring the services of any one of these people, though, think about who has the expert's loyalty. Many insurance agents, for example, earn commissions from insurance companies and as a result charge you nothing. This doesn't mean you don't get good—free—financial advice, it just means the agent will be trying to sell you insurance along with the advice. His loyalty goes to his employer. On the other hand, you pay a financial planning adviser or an accountant, and his loyalty is strictly to you. Both kinds of advisers can be very helpful, provided you understand the situation.

Before getting involved with any financial expert, check his or her references. The best reference, of course, comes from a satisfied friend. You can also casually ask the person the first time you meet him about his background and training. Ultimately, though, before you trust anyone with your money, you should like him. Personal chemistry accounts for a lot in choosing anyone with whom you will have financial dealings.

The one adviser a free-lancer is most likely to have is an accountant or an accounting service. It is strongly suggested that you have an accountant do your taxes. In fact, if you feel you cannot handle the records systems that have been described in this chapter, you can hire an accounting service to set up a record system for you, but it is expensive. A one-time setup will cost $200 to $500. Alternately, the accountant who handles your taxes may be willing to help you set up a records system for a small fee. When you are negotiating with him, remind him that any system you work out is only to his benefit since he goes over the records at the end of the year, anyway.

SETTING UP YOUR OWN BENEFITS PACKAGE

The last step in securing your financial future is to set up your own benefits package. Remember all those things you used to get gratis from your employer—pension, health and major medical insurance, life insurance? Well, you can arrange all these things and anything else you may need for yourself. Try to make arrangements before you start free-lancing.

Many free-lancers say they cannot afford insurance, and some free-lancers do not know how to go about getting this kind of protection. Admittedly, it isn't always a hassle-free chore, particularly if you need many different kinds of insurance or must purchase insurance from several different agents, but you *must* have insurance coverage. Simply hoping that nothing will happen to you is irresponsible—and that is always when trouble strikes.

When working on this step in financial planning, think of yourself as putting together a benefits package. Basically, you will need some health and major medical coverage; disability, something you may not have considered before; professional coverage; and a retirement plan. Here are some hints on how to go about planning a benefits package:

1. List all the ways you can possibly suffer loss.

2. List possible kinds of insurance. If you don't know what you need or what it is called, read on.

3. Talk to several brokers. It is worthwhile to shop around on insurance.

4. For convenience, try to find one broker who can provide several kinds of coverage. For example, one broker might provide renter's or homeowner's insurance, liability, and business interruption insurance. But if you find that buying from several brokers is cheaper than buying from one, then go that route. Also look for insurance buys provided by groups to which you belong. For example, one free-lancer buys disability insurance from her university alumnae group.

5. Do not conceal anything from the broker when you discuss your needs with him. This is silly and only hurts you in the long run.

6. Once you have policies, do everything possible to keep losses to a minimum to avoid the risk of cancellation. You do not have the protection you had when you were part of a large group.

7. Store your policies in a safe place, perhaps a safe or a lockbox. If you rent a lockbox for this purpose, it is tax deductible.

The following sections offer information on the individual components of your benefits package.

Social Security

Whether you realize it or not, you already own one insurance policy—one that you have no choice about owning. That is social security. As a free-lancer, you must pay the share of social security you always paid, plus an additional amount, which is not quite as much as your former employer paid. In 1981, you paid 9.3 percent of your income up to a maximum of $29,700 toward social security. The amount is scheduled to climb in coming years. Social security is called the Self-Employment Tax, and you declare it on a Schedule SE.

Since you are going to become more aware of the pinch this insurance policy makes on your pocketbook, you might be interested in knowing what your benefits are:

- Full retirement benefits from age 65 or from age 62 with a reduced level of benefits.

- Survivors' benefits for spouse, children, and elderly dependent parents.

- Disability for emotional or physical problems, under certain conditions. Disability must be long-term, for example, and you must be ill for five months before you can begin to collect benefits.

- Hospital insurance for people over age 65 and persons who have been disabled longer than twenty-four months.

To qualify for social security, you must have worked a minimum amount of time. Eligibility is determined by quarters of a year worked, and as of 1981, the minimum number of quarters will be forty, which amounts to ten years.

Check your social security record every few years, especially if you have job-hopped very much, which many free-lancers do before settling into free-lancing. You can do this by filling out a postcard that is available from your regional social security office. You will be sent a summary of the earnings credited to you. The government only has to go back three years to correct an error except where there has been a complete omission in reporting on the part of an employer. There are exceptions to this three-year deadline, however, and older errors do get corrected, but make it easy on yourself and check regularly.

A typical pattern is for free-lancers to retire later than other workers, so you will be interested to learn that you are eligible for a 1 percent increase in benefits for every year you work and do not claim benefits from age 65 to 71.

Retirement Accounts

Social security was never intended to be anyone's primary retirement plan, and with the chunk inflation is taking out of everyone's money, including that of the government, it will for most people be little more than a supplementary plan. Therefore, you need to set up a retirement plan in addition to social security. Two kinds of personal retirement plans have come into existence in the past few years, and the 1982 tax reforms make setting up your own retirement plan easier and more advantageous than ever before. Banks and other institutions will be establishing plans to accommodate these new accounts, which are called Individual Retirement Accounts (IRAs) and Keoghs.

Prior to 1982 only people not covered by a pension plan at work could set up an Individual Retirement Account; now anyone can establish one and put up to $2,000 in it each year. More advantageous to a free-lancer, though, are the special retirement accounts called Keoghs. On income earned up until 1982, a free-lancer could put away 15 percent of his income up to a maximum of $7,500; after 1982, a free-lancer could put away 7 percent of his income up to a maximum of $15,000. This amount is substantial enough so that it will probably reduce the number of individuals who incorporate in order to take advantage of the higher rate available in corporate retirement plans.

The best part about retirement accounts is that the money you put in them is subtracted from your income before your taxes are figured. The money is tax-free until you reach age 59½, when you are eligible to start withdrawing it from the account. At that time, presumably, if you have retired you will be in a lower bracket. You need not take any money out of an account until age 70½, at which time you can no longer add money to the account, and you are subject to a 50 percent tax penalty if you are not withdrawing money.

Setting up a retirement account is no more complicated than opening a bank account. Money can be put almost anywhere except in insurance policies, collectibles, and investments made with borrowed funds. When considering what kind of account to establish, look for (1) safety and (2) a steady yield over the years. Banks, brokerage houses, savings and loan institutions, insurance companies, and investment management companies all will be offering retirement plans.

You will probably have to pay a setup fee and an annual custodial fee, but these expenses are deductible and fairly small. As of this writing, for example, Oppenheimer charges $30 a year to maintain a fund; Merrill, Lynch, $25 and $40, depending upon the fund you select; and Fidelity charges $10 for each mutual fund in which you invest money.

A new plan must be set up by December 31 in which you claim the tax deduction. With an established plan, you can put money into an account any time until you pay your taxes, including any extensions you ask for, which usually means April 15 and June 15.

You can also switch your money from one account to another in order to take advantage of changing rates of return. This is called rolling-over an account. You can also use the money at any age if you are disabled. You can rollover an account as often as you like if you send it directly from one institution to another. If the amount goes to you you can only rollover the account once a year in this manner, and you must reinvest it within sixty days. Should you get into a cash flow bind, this could be a way to get your hands on some ready cash—temporarily. You could have the money in your fund sent to you directly, use it until you get in the money you are owed, and then, providing you put it into a new account within sixty days, incur no penalty.

If you use the money prior to retirement, you must pay a 10 percent penalty, and the money also will be taxed as income. There is one time, however, when you might want to put some money into a retirement account, knowing that you will withdraw it and pay the penalty. According to one accountant, a free-lancer could actually come out ahead on his Keogh account if he anticipated a low income one year and had a fairly sizable one the year before—sizable enough so he could afford to place some of the money in a Keogh or IRA. The 10 percent penalty, plus the reduced tax bracket he would be in as a result of earning less money during the year he lived on his savings, would be lower than if he had paid taxes on the large sum. This maneuver, which can work well for any free-lancer who accrues large chunks of money in one year and then lives on it the next year, must be planned carefully. You should probably consult with an accountant who is familiar with your financial situation before doing this.

Health Insurance

The most immediate and needed insurance is to protect your health. The first thing you should do when you are thinking about free-lancing—or if you have been fired or discharged from your job for any reason—is to see if your former employer can carry you for a few months on his insurance. This way, you can still benefit from the lower group rates, and you have some time to shop around and set yourself up with new insurance.

When looking for major medical and other kinds of health insurance (what you need depends upon how healthy you are, a judgment you must make), look for groups you can join that offer insurance as a benefit. Many professional groups and unions offer their members an opportunity to obtain group insurance at rates that are somewhat lower than individual rates. Usually, membership in these insurance plans opens up only once or twice a year, so you must be prepared to take advantage of them when they are available, and you may have to buy other coverage in the interim.

If you must buy an individual policy, the rates will be higher than if you belonged to a group. There are several things you can do to cut the cost of your health insurance. First, be sure to shop around. Rates vary, as does coverage. Consider what you can live with and without in terms of health insurance. For example, if you are in therapy, you will need a policy that covers it. If you are not in therapy, and can safely predict that you won't be for a while, then you can buy much less expensive coverage that does not cover therapy. Also consider opting for a high deductible. If you are healthy and rarely see a physician, you can probably go with a $500 deductible rather than a $100 or $200. Many free-lancers use a high deductible to cut insurance costs.

Finally, give some thought to joining a prepaid health-care plan in lieu of buying major medical insurance. Often membership in such a group is offered through the same organizations that offer group insurance rates. A prepaid health plan is excellent for anyone with ongoing medical problems that require frequent attention. It is also good for a free-lancer on a budget because it means that you receive all your medical care at a prepaid price, which is usually lower than group insurance rates. When calculating whether or not you will save money with a prepaid health-care plan, you should also take into account how much you typically spend each year for routine medical examinations because these will not cost extra with a health plan. With regular group or individual major medical insurance, you must pay for routine office visits to physicians. The chart on page 82 compares the benefits of prepaid health care plans with the benefits of major medical insurance.

Health Maintenance Organization	Major Medical
Limited selection of physicians from among those on HMO staff. Freedom to switch from one physician to another if you want to.	Choose any private physician you want to.
No deductible.	Usually has deductible.
No coinsurance. Pays full medical expenses with few exceptions stated in policy.	Eighty-twenty coinsurance after deductible. This means if you hold two policies, you cannot collect double for long or serious illness; one policy pays 80 percent; the other, 20 percent.
Enrollment limited to geographical area in which you live to be a member. You are reimbursed for emergency care when you are traveling outside the area and need to see a physician.	You are covered anywhere.
Must use affiliated hospitals.	Can use own or physician's hospital.
Lower rates, particularly for family coverage.	Higher rates.

Disability Insurance

Disability insurance pays you a set fee when you are hospitalized or unable to work. Some policies only pay you for the days when you are actually hospitalized; others pay for days when you do not work. Disability covers you in the event of serious illness; it does not automatically pay you for occasional sick days as your former employer probably did.

There are several kinds of disability insurance, and you will need to discuss them and your needs with an insurance agent. Disability insurance can sometimes be purchased through a group. One writer purchased a policy from her college alumni group that pays her $50 a day for every day she is hospitalized—another reason you are wise to look carefully at the benefits of any possible group you can join. She pays approximately $45 a year for this coverage. A therapist with a private practice spends nearly $1,000 annually for far more comprehensive coverage that would pay him full salary should he fall ill.

Many free-lancers put off purchasing disability because they feel they cannot afford it, and often they are correct if they want to purchase full coverage for their salaries. But if you want to find a policy that will pay your monthly bills and cover your rent, with diligent searching you can probably find some kind of suitable coverage. If you do decide not to purchase disability coverage when you start free-lancing, it is still something you should reconsider every year when you review your benefits package.

Disaster Insurance

In addition to major medical health insurance, disaster insurance is probably the next most important coverage. The most common disaster insurance you can buy is fire insurance, although other forms of protection can often be added for a small fee. There are several things to keep in mind when shopping for disaster insurance:

- It can be purchased whether you own or rent.

- Try to buy as comprehensive a policy as possible.

- Especially try to get some kind of liability coverage; this is usually offered with a homeowner's or renter's insurance policy. If people will be coming to your home frequently for business purposes, you may even need more than the minimal amount most renter's or homeowner's policies supply. Get as much liability as you can afford.

- Before buying a policy, find out how you will be compensated: (1) cash value of property at time of loss; (2) repair or replacement with goods of similar quality; (3) take all property at appraisal value or agreed upon value and reimburse you for losses.

- Remember that even if you own several policies, you can collect only on one at a time. For example, if you own two renter's policies and you are robbed of $500 worth of goods, the policies will share the costs of your damages rather than each paying you $500. If you conceal or misrepresent property or try to make two policies pay for one loss, your policies may be rendered void, and you may have trouble getting this kind of insurance again.

- If you file a claim, take extra care to avoid future losses, or you may find yourself paying an unusually high monthly rate.

- When you do suffer a loss or damage, file immediately for damages.

- If you and your agent disagree regarding your losses, resolve them through appraisal procedures. In any event, you should have a list of what you own and even take pictures, if at all possible.

- If you have anything of unusual value, such as furs, jewelry, or antiques, then you should have them professionally appraised and attach a special rider, which can be purchased for only a few dollars extra to cover these items.

As with any insurance, you should review your coverage and shop around periodically. Don't assume once you have purchased insurance that you are set. The premiums will probably go up every year, and that should be enough to make you shop around periodically to be sure you get the lowest possible price for the coverage you need.

You may find that you need special protection to cover the loss from disaster of accounts, deeds, invoices, evidences of debt, manuscripts, photographs, equipment, or other similar properties, and money and securities. Your disaster policy may not cover these items. If this is the case, it is necessary to purchase this kind of coverage separately. In addition, you may need or want to purchase crime insurance to cover the loss of anything else associated with your work.

If you live in a high-crime area and cannot get insurance without paying a very high premium, look into federal crime insurance. Call an insurance agent or the State Insurance Commissioner to get information on this special program.

Business Interruption Insurance

This is a kind of insurance you may be able to purchase only when you are a successful free-lancer, but it is worth looking into every time you review your benefits package to see whether or not you can afford it. Depending upon the kind of policy you buy, such insurance can cover fixed expenses and profits; it can also cover business interruptions if fire or other disasters close you down; it can cover you if a supplier closes down, and this interrupts your business. Some policies are written to cover your extra expenses if your office is damaged but not closed down. You can also get a business interruption policy to cover you if your business is interrupted by failure or interference of power, water, or heat.

WHEN YOU HAVE MONEY
TO SPARE

Yes, with careful financial planning, the day will come when you will have some extra money on hand. Your bills will be paid, your rent will be covered, and the work will still be coming in. For many free-lance writers, for example, sizable chunks of money come in when they contract to write a book. When this happens, you need to think of something to do with money between the time it arrives at your office and the time you need to start drawing on it to meet expenses. No small or large business ever lets money sit idle that could be earning interest, and your independent operation should not be an exception to this rule.

The simplest thing to do is to put the money into a savings account, where it will only earn about 5½ percent. A smarter thing to do is to look for some kind of easily liquidated, high-interest place to put your money. As of this writing, money funds are an excellent place to stash extra capital, and if you have enough money to meet the requirements for minimum deposits, you might consider a six-month certificate of deposit, commonly called a C.D. Often, money funds and C.D.s require a larger amount of money than many free-lancers can part with all at once, and you must lock up your money for six months or more. Before ruling these out, though, consider merging funds with a friend. While banks don't advertise this as a possibility, there are no regulations to stop you from banding together with one or more friends to pool your money for investment purposes. Just be sure you set up the arrangement in a businesslike manner and that you put your agreement in writing.

To learn more about these ways to invest money, contact stockbrokers, bankers, and other financial institutions. The advertisements in the financial section of a newspaper will give you many leads.

THE IMPORTANCE OF GOOD
FINANCIAL HABITS

Many free-lancers have a tough time understanding why they should take care of themselves financially. It seems to go against their grain in some way. Yet if you truly want to be a successful free-lancer—and if you want the independence that comes from earning enough money to live well—you will concern yourself with financial matters. Many free-lancers who have always felt they had no head for financial dealings are often surprised to learn that they are adept at this once they learn what to do and how to do it. One thing is certain: If you want to be a successful free-lancer, and that means anything from existing above a mere subsistence level to earning enough to live very well, then you must learn as much as you possibly can about the financial end of free-lancing.

Free-lancers and the IRS
5

Although mail can be the highlight of a free-lancer's day, one kind of mail rings terror in the heart and sends the blood pressure soaring, and that is anything from the IRS. Fears about the IRS—aside from the healthy ones related to the fact that the IRS does indeed have considerable power over you—are something that free-lancers cannot afford. Neither is ignorance, another cloak in which many free-lancers like to wrap themselves. Consider the case of the free-lance editor, in business only a couple of years, who insisted that she did not have to pay taxes quarterly, despite the protests of her friends that she did indeed have to pay in this way. Irritated by the suggestion that she might be breaking the law, she kept repeating that she knew nothing about the law; after all, the IRS still sent her the short form to use for filing taxes. After five years of free-lancing—some more and some less, which may account for the IRS's not catching up with her sooner—a bill arrived for several hundred dollars. It was a penalty for failure to pay her taxes quarterly. Undaunted, and sure that her pleas of ignorance would get her off the hook, she made an appointment with an IRS agent. The agent listened somewhat sympathetically and then suggested that she break up her rather large bill into smaller quarterly payments—in addition, that is, to the quarterly tax payments she would now be required to make. The point is, no matter how much you may fear and dislike the IRS, taxes, and matters financial, you cannot as the owner of your own small business afford not to understand your tax situation. Even if you hire an accountant or a financial planner, you still need to know what your tax situation is. You need to know what records you must keep, what you can deduct, and when to pay your taxes. This is just smart business policy—and that is what successful free-lancing is all about.

THE IRS AND FREE-LANCERS

The IRS takes a rather dim view of free-lancers. They think free-lancers have an easier time hiding income than do people who work as full-time employees and receive regular paychecks from which sizable chunks of money have already been deducted for taxes. They think free-lancers keep rather sloppy records. (And too often, they have been proven correct on this score.)

The IRS would like to impose a 10 percent withholding tax on all free-lancers. That means that for every paycheck you receive, 10 percent will already have been deducted. (You will still be expected to remit the balance that you may owe on April 15.)

The IRS also would like to tighten the definition of who is and who is not a free-lancer. If you work in an employer's office or exclusively for one client, the IRS would like to change your free-lance status to that of full-time or part-time employee. This would subject you to regular withholding taxes and social security taxes.

Neither of these measures is likely to become law, since

congressional approval is necessary for a standard 10 percent deduction, and tightening the definition of free-lancers is one of those complicated ideas that would be difficult to carry out. For example, suppose you lost your free-lance status because you had one employer but you still worked at home? Would you also lose your office deduction? But how could you take it as a full-time employee? This is just one complicated issue that arises when the IRS tried to limit the scope of free-lancers' work lives.

While the IRS is unlikely to get either of these measures passed, it does have great power over you. The first rule of getting along with the IRS, in fact, is never to ignore them. File your taxes, and if at all possible, file them on time. And read on to see what the IRS can do to verify that you have filed the right amount.

When you worked for someone, your employer gave you a W-2 form as a record of earnings and taxes withheld. Any client who pays you more than $600 as a free-lancer in one year must send you a 1099 form. The IRS knows what you earn because it gets copies of your 1099 forms. Because you do not have to attach the 1099s to your tax forms, some free-lancers erroneously think this is a reason to report less income than they actually have earned. For many years, too, most free-lancers and their accountants believed that the IRS did not have the computer capacity to cross-check all the 1099s with the free-lancer returns. This is a hot topic of conversation wherever free-lancers gather in the month of April. The truth is, the IRS almost certainly does have the capacity to do that, witnessed by the fact that they catch people who fail to report interest on savings accounts, for which 1099s are also filed by banks and savings institutions. Whether or not they match 1099s to every single free-lancer every single year is beside the point; if there is anything irregular about your return, or if for any reason you are audited, the IRS will undoubtedly pull your 1099s and match them to your return. And they undoubtedly match some 1099s in order to establish TCMPs, about which you will read more later. The lesson here is very simple: Report your earnings honestly.

Second, the IRS can check the amounts of money that flow through your checking and savings accounts, and these present a fairly accurate record of how much money you have earned—and spent—throughout the year. The IRS can enter a safe deposit box with a court order. Between these two powers, there is not much you can hide from the IRS, nor should you try to hide much from them.

On the other hand, the IRS is not out to get you simply because you are a free-lancer, and there is no reason to live in fear of the IRS just because you happen to free-lance for a living. Thousands of free-lancers take every single deduction to which they are entitled, year after year, and never hear from the IRS. As you will learn later, your chances of being audited are neither so high nor so arbitrary as you might imagine. And you certainly will not be audited simply because you free-lance.

Even stranger than people who will risk doing something fraudulent to avoid paying taxes are those who resist taking every single deduction to which they are entitled. More than one free-lancer reported not taking a deduction for a home office because he knew the IRS was cracking down on them. Some free-lancers are afraid to take all the deductions they might because they think doing so will invite the IRS to audit them. Keeping a low profile, they believe, is their best defense against the IRS. But taking deductions to which you are entitled does not put you at any higher risk. This is a case of confusing tax evasion with tax avoidance. Tax avoidance is legal and desirable. Russell C. Harrington, former commissioner of the IRS, has stated, "Tax evasion is illegal. Tax avoidance isn't. Every taxpayer has a right to adjust his affairs so that he minimizes his tax liability."

YOUR TAX STATUS AS A FREE-LANCER

Three things about your tax situation change when you begin to free-lance. First, you must pay quarterly. Second, you must pay your own social security taxes. And third, you will probably need some assistance in filing your taxes. Some free-lancers merely consult with a tax accountant every few years to become aware of new tax rulings, then continue to file their own returns, using anything new they may have learned. Other free-lancers are more than happy to turn over all their tax and income records to a good accountant. If you fall into the latter category, though, remember that you still must be an active participant. It is *your* taxes that the accountant is handling.

Paying Quarterly

Let's begin with that fact that you must pay your income taxes on a quarterly basis. This is required of all businesses, corporations, and self-employed persons. It requires a simple calculation. Actually, you estimate your tax bill for the entire year, divide by four, and make those payments. On April 15, like everyone else, you figure out what you have actually made and settle up with the IRS, either by paying the remainder of what you owe them or by getting a refund because you have paid too much. Quarterly income tax payments are due on April 15, when you also owe the unpaid amount on your previous year's tax bill; on June 15; on September 15; and on January 15. Most free-lancers grumble about how inconvenient the dates are, but most free-lancers would not find any other dates any more convenient, and there is nothing you can do to change them, anyway.

The guidelines on paying quarterly taxes are specific. You must pay 80 percent of your annual tax bill or risk a 20 percent penalty for underpayment. The same penalty applies if you do not pay quarterly. There is one loophole: If your current payments equal your tax bill for the preceding year, then you are safe. This means, for example, that if you paid $1,500 in federal income taxes in 1982, even though you will owe $2,000 in 1983, you need not pay more than $1,500 before April 15, 1983, but you must still pay quarterly if you want to avoid a penalty.

If you do not file at all, you may be fined 5 percent of the tax due, plus 5 percent for each month you do not pay, up to 25 percent. If you file but do not pay, the penalty is considerably less—½ percent per month. (Both penalties are in addition to the 20 percent penalty for failure to pay quarterly or for underestimation of your quarterly taxes.) Occasionally, a free-lancer who is in a cash flow bind will simply skip filing, but this is silly when you consider that the penalty for nonpayment is so much less than the penalty for nonfiling. This makes the situation regarding a free-lancer's taxes pretty clear: Try to pay the IRS what you owe when you owe it because underpayment or failure to pay quarterly will only increase the size of your tax bill.

On the other hand, do not pay the IRS more than you owe. Because of the financial insecurity of free-lancing, you may be tempted to apply an income tax return toward next year's tax bill. This, you think, will help to ease the cash flow crunch that accompanies tax-paying time. It sounds like a good idea, and it may help you sleep better at night, but you pay a price for doing this. Consider that someone is earning interest on money all the time. If you pay the IRS in advance or give them more than they are owed, they, rather than you, will earn interest on your tax money. If you take the money from last year's return or estimate your earnings a little on the low side, then you will earn the interest on that money. And you will have the use of the money throughout the year.

Paying Social Security Tax

The second situation that changes when you become a free-lancer is your social security bill. Your former employer picked up part of the tab for your social security. As a self-employed person, you pay your own way. You must pay social security if you have a net profit of more than $400. (Net profit for tax purposes is determined by subtracting the amount of operating expenses from gross profit.) In recent years, social security has been climbing, and it is scheduled to climb still more in the future.

To pay your social security tax, you first figure out your federal income tax bill. Based on your net income, you figure how much social security you owe. You use a special form entitled Schedule SE to file your social security tax, although you write one check to cover your social security and your federal income tax.

When to File

The best time to file your quarterly tax payments, including social security, is as close to the deadlines as possible. This is especially helpful on the April 15 payment. Persons who expect a refund often file early in January so they can get the refund as soon as possible, but this may not be the wisest course of action. If you file April 15, your return arrives in the huge mound of other returns, since most Americans pay right on the deadline. That is when the burden of work on the IRS is highest. And while you won't be overlooked if you have done something glaringly wrong, your return inevitably will be less closely scrutinized than it would be if you mailed it very early or, for that matter, very late.

Getting Help

The third and final thing that changes for you is that you probably do need some professional tax assistance. You can stumble along by yourself for several years, and you probably won't make any major mistakes, especially if you have an aptitude for figures. On the other hand, there just might be some loophole or some form to fill out that you have not considered, and that's where a good accountant can advise you.

One artist who never cared much about money until he started working for himself reported that he managed quite well for five years without an accountant, but, as he found out the first year he went to one, he got along better with the accountant's help: "I prided myself on having become a bit of a tax sharpie. But I thought I would check in with an accountant just to see what I could learn. Actually, I imagined I would go one year to pick his brain and never return. What I found out was that I was basically doing everything right, but I had been taking my art books as a straightforward deduction whereas he decided that I should depreciate them as a professional library. He also introduced me to an energy credit that I got for insulating my studio. He was worth the money, and I've gone back every year since."

Another place you can turn to for tax advice is the IRS, although most taxpayers have a healthy, natural resistance to doing so. It makes sense, since their goal is to get your money, that you wouldn't let them be the ones to figure out what you owed them. On the other hand, if you have a simple question that can be handled over the phone, the IRS does provide free tax advice. One free-lance graphic designer reported her dilemma over having moved from Chicago, where cab drivers readily gave receipts, to New York, where they never seemed to have receipts, let alone a piece of scrap paper or a pen. She checked with other free-lancers, heard many differing stories, and finally called the IRS regional office. She learned that the IRS realized that New York cabbies were not forthcoming with receipts and didn't expect them during an audit.

Two problems arise from taking advice from the IRS: Their advice is not binding, and you can call five different agents and get five different answers. There is a movement under way to let you record advice from the IRS, and while this would help somewhat, it still doesn't make the advice binding. Therefore, take even what you hear from an IRS agent with a grain of salt.

Overall, though, your best bet is to find a good accountant—possibly even one who free-lances himself. Finding the right accountant can be tricky, and many free-lancers have horror stories about what their accountants put them through. Some free-lancers report their accountants' reluctance to let them deduct their home offices, even though they have no other base of operations. Another free-lancer noted that the first accountant he saw let him deduct almost nothing and insisted that he open a retirement account before he would handle his taxes. Another free-lancer's accountant refused to let her deduct her home office because most of her mortgage payments were interest, and he said this would be a double deduction. It might be if all the payments were interest, which was not the case. There was something left over, and she should have been deducting a home office. These few examples should suffice to convince you that you have to know a little about your tax situation even to find a good accountant. You don't want an accountant who plays so fast and free with his clients that they are frequently audited, nor do you want one who discourages you from deductions you have every right to take. You do want an accountant who knows every single loophole and who will encourage you to reduce your tax bill in every possible way. It's a nice bonus to find an accountant who also can give you some basic financial planning advice, such as suggestions for the kinds of records you should keep or ideas about where to put a chunk of capital that you don't need to live on right away.

A story is passed around every year at tax time that the IRS has a list of accountants whom they consider to be slightly shady, and that their clients are audited with greater frequency than are the clients of accountants who are not on the list. The IRS denies having such a list, although they admit they have the capacity to pull all the returns done by any one accountant. Whether or not the IRS has such a list doesn't matter, since you probably cannot get your hands on it anyway. What does matter is that they do watch accountants who consistently go further than the law permits. So while you may be tempted to find the sleaziest accountant around and let him do whatever he wants with your taxes, think twice. You are the one who ultimately is responsible, and the accountant is liable to be known to the IRS for the wrong reasons. Your accountant will go with you if you are called for an audit, and he will argue your case, but you pay the bill, if any—and you also pay the accountant for accompanying you on an audit. So check out an accountant carefully before engaging him to handle your income taxes.

Presumably, this can all work in reverse, too. If you have an accountant who has a flawless reputation with the IRS, he will be less likely to encounter close scrutiny since the IRS will know from years of seeing his returns that they are well done.

As your tax situation gets more complicated, you can also reduce your chances of an audit by using a professional tax preparer. Doing so will cause fewer raised eyebrows in the IRS office. Complicated returns prepared without professional help are scrutinized carefully because the IRS knows from experience that they often contain errors.

Here are some things to think about as you look for an accountant:

- Word-of-mouth is the best way to find an accountant. Satisfied people love to pass on the names of their accountants.

- Get someone who does returns for lots of free-lancers, preferably in your field. That means, if you are a writer, get an accountant who works with a lot of writers; if you are an artist, get an accountant who works with lots of artists.

- Ask the accountant for his credentials when you make the initial phone call to talk to him. Find out what professional associations he belongs to. Remember, though, that he need not necessarily be a Certified Public Accountant, a credential many people look for, but can be certified in tax preparation by the IRS.

- Find out, too, what he charges and how much time he thinks will be required to do your taxes.

WORKING WITH AN ACCOUNTANT

Once you have found an accountant, there are some things you can do to make his and your work easier. For the kind of attention you need, you will probably pay an accountant by the hour rather than on retainer. In small rural communities, this hourly fee may be as low as $15 or $20; in large urban areas, it often runs $40 or $50. Therefore, it is to your advantage to reduce the amount of time you spend with your accountant, and you should also have some idea how much time your accountant expects to spend on your business. Shelley Martin, an accountant who has done thousands of returns for free-lancers and small businesses in New York City, reports that one to two hours is the average amount of time she spends on any one job, although once she spent eighteen hours on one very complicated job that required a great deal of research. Martin noted, "When someone shows up and dumps a year's worth of receipts on my desk, I tell him to go right home again and sort them out himself because he will only pay me for the time I spend sorting out those receipts." Rule Number One, then, is to sort your own receipts before you go to the accountant. You need not even take them with you. Just take a list of the totals for your deductions. For example, note what your rent on office or studio space costs monthly, how much utilities are, how much you have spent on supplies, how much on entertainment, and then take these totals to the accountant's office. If you are not sure whether or not an item is deductible, take the figures anyway and let your accountant advise you.

Rule Number Two: Don't make your accountant a co-conspirator. One free-lance nurse recalled the new leather purse she had bought just before she met her accountant for lunch. It was a larger purse than she would need in a different line of work, and with some legitimacy she had decided to declare the purse deductible—it was going to become a briefcase. She gleefully asked her accountant how he liked her new briefcase. He blanched and said, "That's fine if that is what you consider a briefcase; just don't tell me about it or show me." In other words, your accountant does not want to hear about the shades of gray you establish in deductible areas. On the other hand your accountant may subtly let you know that you can deduct more than you have been in a certain area. For example, if you do not keep the best of records and you estimate your annual transportation costs, your accountant may suggest that your deduction could be larger. Listen to such advice and then decide whether or not you feel comfortable following it.

YOUR DEDUCTIBLE LIFE

Now that you have heard what the IRS can do to you, it is time to hear what they can do for you, so to speak. Free-lancer's lives are largely deductible, or they can be that way if they are run on that basis. Always remember, though, that for every dollar you spend on your business, only about one-third is actually saved in income taxes. Most free-lancers are eligible to take far more deductions than they actually do. For example, these are the areas where you can take deductions as a free-lancer:

Rent or mortgage payment for office or studio
Utilities
Real-estate taxes on property used as office or studio
Depreciation on office or studio if owned
Travel for business
Education
Transportation
Membership dues
Publications, newspapers, journals, etc., related to your
    work
State sales tax
Safe deposit rental, if you keep business papers in it
Retirement plans
Moving expenses
Subcontracting
Clothes, if worn specifically for work
Tools and supplies needed to carry out work
General office supplies, including business stationery and
    cards
Postage
Answering service and/or machine
Office equipment
Depreciation on office equipment
Bad debts
Public relations and advertising expenses
Gifts and holiday cards to clients
Legal services

Financial planning services
Entertainment
Insurance
Repair services
Equipment or furniture rental
Printing and copying services
Cleaning services and/or supplies

Of course, you can't write off all your rent unless you rent an office or studio that is separate from your home, nor can you deduct a trip if you do not conduct business while traveling, but surely you can see the possibilities for deductions.

The first thing to remember about deductions is that they must be work-related. For example, a trip must be related to the work you are doing right now. If you travel for ten days, but work only on five of those days, then only five days of your trip are deductible (see exception on page 103). Educational expenses must be used to develop or build skills for work you are currently doing; you cannot deduct classes you take to retrain for another career. Membership dues, too, must not be for social clubs or organizations but must be for legitimate groups related to business or for clubs where you do business entertaining.

Safe and Unsafe Deductions

There are safe and not-so-safe deductions, which means that some deductions are more likely than others to trigger an audit. But if you read the articles and books on taxes that appear annually at tax time, you will quickly realize that most of the major deductions of free-lancers are not particularly safe. Don't worry about this. If you have a right to a deduction, you have nothing to fear from the IRS by taking it.

The classic example of an unsafe deduction is the home office. A few years ago the IRS clamped down on home offices, supposedly because so many teachers were claiming them even though they had offices at school. The IRS obtained a tax ruling to the effect that a home office had to be in a separate room and that it could not be used for any other purpose. No more spreading out a project on the dining room table; for that matter, as far as the IRS was concerned, there would be no more living and working in a studio apartment. When asked about this, one accountant in New York, where thousands of free-lancers live in studio apartments, laughed and said, "I tell my clients to be prepared to throw up a wall if the IRS decides to come and take a look."

Suddenly, not only were free-lancers and their accountants afraid to deduct home offices in studio apartments, but some were frightened to deduct a home office at all, fearing that it alone would trigger an IRS audit.

Unfortunately for free-lancers, the home office is a major deduction, one that no free-lancer should relinquish. Some accountants advise attaching a note to a free-lance return explaining your full-time free-lance status as a reason that you have deducted a home office. Shelley Martin is among those agents who feel that attaching such a note is like attaching a red flag to your return begging an agent to look it over. The point is that full-time free-lancers are entitled to write off their offices, and you should never feel uncomfortable about a deduction to which you are legitimately entitled. Deduct the office. An IRS agent can read your return carefully and figure out that you are a gainfully self-employed free-lancer.

In addition, there is relief in sight for free-lancers who live and work in one room. A recent tax court ruling disallowed the rule that the office had to be in a separate room, although the judge did decide that the space has to be used exclusively for work.

Calculating the Home Office Deduction

When deducting your office in your home, figure the amount you can deduct by counting the number of rooms and dividing by the number used for work, or by calculating floor space and dividing by the amount used for work. For example, if you live in a four-room apartment and use one room for your office, deduct one-fourth of your rent. On the other hand, if you live in a three-room apartment but you work in part of the living room, which is twice as large as the other two rooms, you might deduct one-third. Most accountants assign about one-third of a studio apartment for office space.

Deducting Utilities

Whatever percentage you deduct for the office, take the same percentage for utilities such as electricity and heat. Your phone bill, which is also a utility, is calculated differently. Deduct the percentage you take for other utilities, and always look over your long-distance or local calls that are deductible. If you have a separate business phone, deduct the entire bill for it.

The Business Entertainment Deduction

Another supposedly unsafe deduction is business entertainment. This is one area where you should keep carefully detailed receipts, noting whom you entertained, how or where, and for what purpose or for what job. So far, the IRS acknowledges that people can get together for a meal for business purposes and not discuss business directly. At meals you need not discuss business, but the atmosphere should be conducive to doing so. This means that you can take a potential client to lunch or even dinner not to discuss business but simply to woo him a little and increase the chances of your getting business from him.

Other Deductions

Most of the other deductions are pretty straightforward and safe. Moving expenses, which many people do not know about, are a safe deduction. If you move thirty-five miles or more for business purposes, your expenses are deductible. There is no limit on the cost of the mover, but you must retain your receipt. There is a $3,000 limit on travel and living expenses while you find a new place to live or work, and also for closing costs and legal fees or other miscellaneous expenses. Self-employed persons must remain self-employed for seventy-eight weeks out of the twenty-four months immediately after the move. Deduct moving expenses for the year in which you move.

Other safe deductions are dues to professional organizations, professional journals and magazines or books, a safe deposit box, courses, and tax counseling. Dividends and interest earned on savings accounts, stocks and bonds, and money funds are deductible up to $200 ($400 for couples). These will undoubtedly be safe deductions because the IRS will have a ready means of cross-checking them and because the amounts will be small for most persons.

Barter is deductible, and while the IRS will not challenge you on this if your receipts are in order, they are particularly attuned to it in self-employed persons, who find informal exchanges of their services easy to carry out.

Business travel is a safe deduction if it is well documented. The IRS recognizes six kinds of out-of-town travel that can be deducted: (1) convention travel, (2) business or research travel, (3) travel to seek new clients or work assignments, (4) travel for a temporary assignment away from home, (5) travel to obtain work-related education, and (6) travel as education in itself. When you take a travel deduction, the primary reason for travel must be for work and not for pleasure. But even if you have a few pleasure days tucked in among the business days, you can still deduct this if the primary purpose of your trip was business. For example, if you schedule a business meeting on Friday and then another on Monday, you can deduct your expenses over the weekend. Only your costs for business travel are deductible; your spouse or children can go along, but you cannot write off their expenses. If you travel by car, you can deduct a certain amount per mile (check with recent tax rulings, as this figure changes frequently with inflation); if you take a room or apartment where you must live temporarily for business purposes, you can deduct it—even if your family uses it, but only if it costs what it would have cost had you taken it alone.

In speaking of safe and unsafe deductions, remember that nothing is safe if it is illegal. Also, you should be aware that the IRS, mostly as a result of their own limited manpower, may declare war on a certain deductible one year and on something else a couple of years later. For example, home offices were targets in the Tax Reform Act of 1976, which restricted their use severely; for the past few years the IRS has been looking into tax shelters. Once they have scared enough people away from shady investments in that area, they will move on to something else.

CASHING IN ON CREDITS

Once you have learned what deductions you can take, start looking into possible credits that you may be eligible to claim. For example, if you subcontract, that is, hire someone to work with you or handle your overflow, then you can take a jobs credit if you give them a raise during the year.

There are energy credits; you can deduct 15 percent of the first $2,000 you spend on insulation, storm windows, and other energy-saving devices, including caulking. You can take a 40 percent credit for the first $10,000 you spend on solar, wind, or geothermal equipment. The child-care credit is 20 percent of all job-related child care costs up to $400 for one child, and $800 for two or more. It will probably go up over the years.

Credits are complicated to calculate, and they change frequently. An energy credit obviously is tied to the current interest in saving energy, just as the investment credit is an attempt to help businesses in inflationary times when new equipment may be too expensive to buy. As these credits are phased out, though, others will probably take their place. The child-care credit, for example, could be removed by a presidential administration that did not support the rights of working women. Deciding what credits you qualify for and calculating how to take them is work probably best left to an accountant.

NEW HELP FROM THE TAX REFORM BILL

The 1982 tax reform bill offered some breaks to free-lancers. Because most free-lancers pay taxes at individual as opposed to corporate rates, the personal tax cuts will help, such as those regarding the increased amounts you can put into a retirement plan or the new exemptions on dividends and interest. For those who are incorporated, the corporate tax rates on the first $50,000 in income were reduced 1 percent in 1982 and another 1 percent in 1983.

The biggest tax break for free-lancers, though, may turn out to be the new ruling that permits them to write off the first $5,000 in capital investments without depreciating them. This limit will climb to $10,000 by 1986. One writer who had been eyeing a word processor he thought he could not afford now estimates that it will be $4,000 cheaper to buy than it was before the capital investment write-off went into effect.

WHAT YOU CANNOT DEDUCT

Some deductions that you cannot take may come as surprise to you, and here again, you will need the advice of an accountant. Most free-lancers think they can deduct insurance, but in fact, you can deduct only a portion of the homeowner's or renter's policy that covers your office. You cannot deduct health insurance, even though your past employer probably used to pay for it and you must now buy your own policy. You cannot deduct charitable contributions on a Schedule C; you can deduct them only on your personal income tax form if you do not take the standardized deduction.

Writers, editors, and others in similar fields commonly assume that they can deduct the cost of a bad debt, that is, when someone for whom they contracted to work, and, in fact, did work, refuses to pay them. You cannot deduct the bad debt—except for actual expenses incurred—unless you claimed the income on your return and paid taxes on it, which might be the case if you use the cash-accrual method of accounting.

As mentioned earlier, you cannot deduct classes that are used to help you find a better job or train into a new career. Only those classes that improve the skills you already have can be deducted. An artist who works in stained glass can take classes in stained-glass technique. A business consultant, for example, can deduct psychology and business classes taken to maintain his consulting skills.

KEEPING RECORDS

Apart from the financial records described in chapter 4, which should be part of any well-organized business, you should keep all receipts for items you plan to deduct. An excellent way of obtaining receipts is to use credit cards, especially for business-related meals, office supplies, and other similar expenses that can be easily charged. Ideally, get a business card—American Express, Carte Blanche, or Diner's Club—and use it only, or mostly, for business. Ways of accounting for receipts are described in chapter 4 on financial planning.

TAX PLANNING—WHAT EVEN
THE FREE-LANCER CAN DO

Too many free-lancers feel like such small operators that they refuse to acknowledge that they can do anything about tax planning. And while it is true that you probably will not have extra cash lying around to invest in pork bellies on the commodities market (a notoriously easy way to lose your money, by the way) or even in blue-chip stocks, there are things you can and should do to save on your income taxes. You can also use your money in ways that spell savings for you. The first and most obvious thing is to make sure as much of your life is deductible as possible.

One trade-book editor, who experienced several lean years before starting to earn a comfortable living, made deductible living her philosophy of life, albeit in a small way. She reported, "When I started free-lancing I knew I was going to have to give up some luxuries I had been used to when I had a regular paycheck every month. Even things I had taken for granted, such as going to three or four movies a week, were now reconsidered. I decided that books, a deductible item for me since I edited fiction and nonfiction and had to keep up with the marketplace, would become my major luxury. After all, they were deductible. When I couldn't stand not spending any money frivolously, I bought myself a book. When a few checks came in and I felt rich, I rewarded myself with a book. I could just as easily have gone to a movie or treated myself to an expensive dinner, but I knew the book was deductible and the movie or dinner wasn't." This free-lancer's instincts were right: She opted to spend her money on deductible items where possible. That is the first step to saving money through your taxes. There are also other ways to make your life deductible. If you do take a vacation, see whether there is some way to combine it with business. If you are a writer, find a subject you want to investigate or someone to interview at your destination. Dancers, musicians, and artists can visit galleries and studios and can talk to people about working for them. When you do travel and work, be sure to write letters in advance requesting appointments so you have proof of actually having conducted business.

The last general thing that you can do to plan your tax situation is to time deductions, when possible. If you earned a lot in one year, try to move some of the income ahead to the next year. Do this by asking clients not to pay you until January or do not bill them until then; alternately, do not deposit checks earned until January. If you want to purchase something big, and you don't need it urgently, decide which tax year would be most beneficial for the purchase. Usually you should try to schedule deductions in a year when your income will be especially high. That is when you will need more deductions. If you need more deductions in one year, pay your rent or a mortgage payment for January in December. That way, you will have the benefit of one more payment in that year. Remember, though, that you cannot claim that payment on the next year's income tax.

On the other hand, manipulating deductions in this way can eventually backfire if your income continues to grow every year. Sooner or later, the money you push ahead will catch up with you, so if you expect your income to grow, do not manipulate income and deductions very much.

Income Averaging

Since free-lancers' incomes are sometimes erratic, you may have a year when everything takes off and your earnings double or triple. If this is the case, consider averaging your income. When you average your income, you spread out the large amount you earned in one year over the four preceding years and reduce your tax bite accordingly. Income averaging only works if you earn substantially more in one year than in the four preceding years.

Furthermore, you must elect to average your income. The IRS does not notify you that this is a possibility. If you were eligible to average in one year, but did not know about income averaging, you can file an amended return and income average.

To average, the excess of your adjusted taxable income for the year in which you hope to average must exceed 30 percent of your total base income. Your total base income is what you have earned over the past four years. James Weikart, senior partner of Weikart Tax Associates and the author of a tax-planning newsletter, devised this simple chart to help his clients decide whether or not they are eligible to income average:

		Income		
	Year	You	Total	Spouse
1.	1983			
2.	1979			
	1980			
	1981			
	1982			
	Total '79–'82			
3.	Total '79–'82 ÷ 4			
4.	No. 1 less No. 3			

If the answer you obtain in Number 4 is $3,000 or more on an individual return or for you and your spouse together, then you should look into income averaging. This chart provides only a rough approximation of your eligibility to income-average; obtaining the result you want does not mean that you can, in fact, income-average. Even if you qualify to average your income, it may not reduce your tax bill. The only way income averaging reduces your tax bill is if it causes you to fall into a lower tax bracket than you would be in if you did not average.

If you are planning to average your income yourself, use Schedule G and get yourself a copy of IRS Publication 506, "Computing Your Tax Under the Income Averaging Method." The best thing to do is see your accountant to be sure your optimism over income averaging really translates into a tax savings.

WHAT IF YOU ARE AUDITED?

Assume that the worst has happened: The IRS has called on you to come in and discuss your return with them—in short, you are being audited.

Keep in mind that the chances that this will happen to you are not really very great. The IRS has 19,000 auditors for 93 million returns. In addition, if you file Schedule C, your return is thrown in with all the other Schedule Cs, including some very "big" small businesses.

Until a couple of years ago, even if you free-lanced part-time, you still were included with all the other schedule Cs, which reduced your chances of being audited still more. Now, though, the IRS classifies the Schedule Cs of part-time free-lancers with other individual tax returns rather than with the businesses run by small proprietors.

Understanding how you are chosen for an audit also will help you to see why you are not likely to be audited. The IRS has a computer program that establishes norms for deductions in each income category. For example, if you live in New York and earn $20,000 a year from free-lance income as a design consultant and you spend $4,000 on entertainment, that probably is more than the norm for your occupation and income category. What happens? Your return will be kicked out of the computer. But merely being kicked out of the computer does not mean that you will be audited. It means that your return will be looked over by a clerk, who then flags your return for an audit or passes on it based in part on how much money the IRS is likely to get if they audit you. For example, more audits are done among people earning over $50,000 a year than among those who earn $20,000 or less. This does not mean, however, that if something is glaringly wrong on your return, you will not be audited just because you do not earn very much. If there is something wrong with your return—if a deductible category is unusually high for no apparent reason—the IRS will question you about this and possibly conduct a full-scale audit.

Furthermore, the IRS may randomly choose you for a

Taxpayer Compliance Measurement Program (TCMP). Audits like this are used to establish the norms. If you are selected for a TCMP audit, there is nothing you can do about it except to comply. Most experts who write about TCMPs would like you to be terrified of the prospect. After all, a TCMP does involve a line audit—the IRS agent goes over every single line of your income tax return, and you must justify every single line to the agent. Free-lancers dread this kind of audit because they envision themselves spending days and even weeks meeting with IRS agents while their businesses flounder for lack of direction and guidance. Most free-lancers, though, do not have very complicated businesses, so even if you are selected for a TCMP audit—or any audit—it probably will not take more than a morning or a day of your life. As an aside, a court case is currently pending to force the IRS to make public the norms or categories of deductions, but no decision has been handed down yet, and, of course, the IRS will fight this vigorously.

Experts hint that several things trigger an audit or cause the IRS to question some part of an income tax return. In a sense, you already do one big thing: You free-lance. And since you are not about to stop free-lancing simply to decrease your chances of being audited, then there is no reason to do anything else to decrease your chances. If for some reason you have high expenses in one year, and they are fully receipted, deduct them even if they cause you to be audited, which they probably will not, given the things you have just read regarding the IRS's limited manpower and desire to collect from taxpayers who will earn them a sizable sum of money.

What other things increase your chances of being audited? If any of your deductions are abnormally large, compared to the DIF standards, you may be called in for questioning or possibly an audit. If your income tax refund is high compared to your income, if you work in a business where you could easily be hiding a lot of income, and if you cannot live on what you appear to earn after deductions, then you are a likely candidate to be audited. But all this is a matter of common sense.

The IRS runs about three years behind on any kind of audit. This means that in 1983 free-lancers can expect to receive inquiries and audits on their 1980 taxes. Notices are usually mailed in the fall. Although the IRS can question you for up to 6 years after they suspect you file a fraudulent return (and that is how long you should keep tax records), in reality, if they have not called you within three years of the time you file a return, you are safe.

If you are called for an audit and you can justify your deductions, then you have nothing to fear. Consider the case of the architect who moved his business and residence from southern Florida to New York. The first year he claimed net earnings (post deductions) of $16,000 and a deduction of $7,000 for entertainment expenses to establish his business. He was called for an audit, whereupon he produced detailed receipts covering his entertainment expenses. He walked away unscathed since all his expenses were legitimate. Only when your expenses are not documented do you have anything to fear from the IRS. Simply having a large deduction may be enough to get you audited, but it is not enough to get you in trouble with the IRS.

If you are called for an audit, there are a few things to keep in mind:

- If at all possible schedule the audit for your accountant's office or your office. If your office is in your home, definitely opt for your accountant's office or the IRS office. Most of the time, the audit will be held in the IRS office; that is the usual practice for a small audit.

- For your own peace of mind, don't postpone the meeting, but rather get it over with as quickly as possible.

- If the IRS letter does not specify what areas of your return are being considered, call them and ask. Then take only the records that relate to that area with you. Walking into an IRS audit with all your records when you are only being questioned about one area is an open invitation to the auditor to escalate the audit. If your business equipment expenses are the area in question, take only the receipts for your business equipment expenses and nothing else. If business equipment and entertainment expenses are being questioned, take only those receipts.

- If you are being audited for something relatively minor, you may not even need to take your accountant with you, but if you sense trouble (if your deductions are not well documented) or are especially nervous when faced with authority, then by all means be sure your accountant accompanies you. In fact, your accountant can go as your representative, but since your affairs are under discussion, you would do well to accompany him or her.

- Dress nicely but not richly. If suitable, wear the clothes you wear to work.

- Be polite and straightforward to the agent.

- Do not act defensively; you may only appear cocky. In fact, do not talk a lot or try to make small talk. The agent cannot be warned up to your interests, and he is fully aware that you are nervous.

- Arrive on time.

- Make sure your records are neatly organized. Throwing a bundle of loose receipts on an agent's desk will only annoy him; it will not stop him from meticulously sorting through them with a vengeance.

- Only answer questions. Do not ask them if you can avoid it, and whatever you do, do not volunteer any extra information that might open up another area of your return for audit.

- You need not show your working papers or notes to the agent, which does not mean he won't say, "Here, let me take a look at those." If you are easily intimidated and might hand over your notes, this is all the more reason to have your accountant along with you. In fact, if you have an accountant in tow, the IRS agent probably will not even suggest such things as looking at your notes or reviewing other nonrelated areas of your return unless he has planned in advance to ask you about those areas.

Official IRS publications remind taxpayers that audits are not necessarily anything to be afraid of. The IRS initiates an audit because they want to verify information on your tax return, not because they are out to get you. And many audits come out in the taxpayer's favor—that is, you may walk away with a little more money than you had to start with.

It does not make good business sense for a free-lancer to avoid taking a deduction or to take less than he is entitled to because he is afraid of an IRS audit. The real trick is not to be afraid of the audit.

WHEN YOU ARE QUESTIONED BUT NOT AUDITED

Your chances of getting a letter from the IRS adjusting your tax bill are far greater than your chances of being audited. Such letters usually come from the general offices of the IRS, not the offices where auditors work. You are told what changes are being made in your tax bill and are invited to: (1) sign the letter and remit the amount in question or (2) respond in writing with an explanation.

One free-lancer received a letter from the IRS stating that she had underpaid her taxes by approximately $5,000 and asking her to remit an additional $1,500 in taxes and penalties. Once she recuperated from the shock, she began to go over her records. Since she knew she had not underpaid her taxes by that or any other amount, she soon found the IRS's errors and wrote a letter explaining why she did not owe that amount. The IRS sent a return letter acknowledging her explanation and accepting it.

Although practically no one would be so intimidated by the IRS that he or she would sign on a dotted line and consent to so large a tax increase, many free-lancers are enough afraid of the IRS that when they receive letters asking for smaller amounts, they are often so relieved that the amount is small and that they are not being audited that they remit the money. Never let yourself be intimidated so easily. Anytime the IRS questions you about any amount, no matter how large or how small, double-check your records to see if you really owe the amount. Never sign or agree to anything until you have checked it to be sure the request is accurate. The IRS can and frequently does make mistakes, and many of those mistakes are on free-lancers' tax returns, which may be a natural result of the fact that their returns are not so routine as the average taxpayers' are.

TAXES AND TALKING SHOP

Taxes inevitably are a favorite topic of free-lancers, like everyone else, especially around April 15. While there are some benefits to be gained from comparing notes on your tax situation or on possible deductions, you are better off not discussing the specifics of your individual tax situation with anyone. Free-lancing, like any business, is competitive, and in some creative fields, the competition becomes intense—and a friendly competitor just might decide to turn on you. One particularly hostile way to do this is to report anything you have said to the IRS, which does have paid informers. The IRS has about seven thousand paid informers, and they are paid an average of about $700 each. Most informers are exes— ex-wives, ex-husbands, ex-friends, and ex-colleagues. Obviously, there will be trusted colleagues with whom you feel confident discussing your tax situation, but in general remember that what people do not know about you, they cannot use against you.

GOING TO TAX COURT

If an audit does not go well and you feel you have been treated unfairly, you can sue the IRS in tax court. For sums of less than $5,000 you do not need a lawyer and can argue your case yourself. Decisions handed down by the tax courts have checked the power of the IRS, and if you have not been treated justly, there is no reason to think that a decision will go against you.

In closing, keep in mind that free-lancers are no more vulnerable to the IRS than other individuals are, but rather, their tax situations are more complicated. That means there is more room for error. As a free-lancer, you should know as much as possible about this part of your business and to seek good advice from an expert on your tax situation. Your tax situation is too intricately entwined with your cash flow to do otherwise.

Selling
Yourself

6

Selling yourself is the hardest part of free-lancing, as every free-lancer interviewed for this book agreed. No one likes to do it very much, and many free-lancers dread it. It's a special bugaboo for new free-lancers, who feel insecure and scared in general about their new ventures. But when you free-lance, you are the product. Often you are the only thing you have to sell—and with few exceptions, such as those free-lancers who have agents or representatives—you are the person who does the selling. Take heart, though. Selling yourself does get easier once you have learned how to do it and as you get more experience. And fortunately most free-lancers quickly build up repeat business and also begin to get referrals, which means they can spend less time making cold calls and soliciting business.

DEVELOPING THE RIGHT ATTITUDE

In order to sell anything, you need contacts. These are either prospective buyers or leads toward prospective buyers. In this chapter, you will learn how to find your customer, whatever service you are selling, and you will learn how to sell yourself to that customer.

The methods most commonly used to sell are personal contact, advertising, and display. Since free-lancers essentially sell services, display—as in decorated windows and flashing signs—are of little use. Advertising helps somewhat, depending upon the nature of your business, but if you are on a tight budget, you can probably get along without it or spend very little on it. Advertising is discussed in chapter 10. The sales method most frequently used by free-lancers is personal contact. You call someone or write him. You personally solicit his business.

One advantage of the personal contact method of sales is that it is cheap, especially for the beginner who may have little else to do with his or her time. It costs very little to make a phone call or mail a letter. An appointment that lasts twenty minutes is, relatively speaking, inexpensive.

Although free-lancing does depend upon personal contact, this does not imply intimacy. Too many free-lancers come on like puppies, indicating a willingness to chat about anything and everything on the phone, having forgotten their days in an office and how overcrowded they could be. Often, too, the new free-lancer, feeling a little isolated and having trouble getting used to the days alone, is unnecessarily hurt when someone does not have time to talk or abruptly ends a meeting or phone conversation. Don't let yourself fall victim to these feelings. Keep in mind the days when you worked in an office and viewed phone calls and meetings as unnecessary interruptions of your busy day. Friendships can and probably will develop between you and some of your clients (one of the pleasures of free-lancing is the open-ended opportunity for finding and making new friends), but this will happen over time. Meanwhile, as a new free-lancer, it is more important for you to learn how to accept and maintain the degree of professional distance you need to run your business. Ways to go about doing this are also discussed later in this chapter.

When you first begin selling yourself, it will seem very strange to you. Making and using contacts is like your first day on a new job, except that this is something you will have to do over and over throughout your free-lance career. At first your goal will be to establish contact and to try to build a working relationship. Your ultimate goal, though, is to get work, or possibly to get an appointment to discuss future work.

In a sense, free-lancing works just the opposite of working as an employee. As an employee, the longer you work for someone, the greater your chances of staying on. As a free-lancer, you do not have this security. While you will have regular customers who will use you over and over, each job is new and separate from the last. And since the employer does not have to fire you but can merely stop calling you, as a free-lancer, you are always being tested. Bill Cook, a playwright who free-lances as a typesetter, remarked, "If you free-lance, you have to be very good at your job. If you're very good at it, then you keep working. You're not let go when other people are. And even if an employer really doesn't like to have free-lancers working for him, he'll keep you on." Free-lance editor Sharon Kapnick commented: "I think you have to be really good. I try to treat each job as if it were the first job—and the only job—for a client, and as if my life depended upon it."

FINDING CLIENTS

If you are thinking about free-lancing, you probably already have an area or profession in which you will work. More specifically, though, when you begin to seek work assignments, you have to pinpoint which persons or companies are likely to need the specific services you offer. When one woman decided to make the switch from teaching to free-lance editing, her long-term goal was to write for textbook companies, but she correctly sensed that this was not an entry-level position, even with her teaching background. After talking with free-lance editors, she decided that her best bet was to solicit copy-editing and proofreading. She then turned to *Literary Market Place*, the bible and phone directory of the publishing business. She also studied the ads in *Publishers Weekly* to see which publishers were likely to need free-lance copy-editors. She called trade-book publishers first and was quickly rewarded with several assignments. Eventually, as her business and her self-confidence grew, she began to approach textbook publishers for copy-editing and proofreading. As she built her contacts in that area, she began to talk to them about doing some writing. That kind of work came in slowly, but she was eventually given an assignment to write some exercises for lower-grade workbooks. That led to still another assignment. She found that her new area of expertise was growing, thanks to referrals. Her success, though, is largely attributable to the fact that she found the right place to enter her field, pinpointed a list of prospective clients, and went after them rather than wasting her time (and prospective clients' time) with a scattershot approach.

Another free-lancer, who went through a similar experience when he started, made this suggestion: "Sit down and write out a paragraph describing your prospective clients—who will need you and why, how often they will need you, who will be best able to pay you well. Then turn to trade directories and publications and use your own contacts to find those potential employers."

Barbara Zimmerman, the only person in New York to free-lance in copyright and permissions, worked hard to carve out that niche after she had settled on publishing as the general field in which she was qualified to free-lance. "I don't know where I found out that nobody did what I do free-lance, but I decided permissions and copyright was a possibility. I started by writing a series of 300 to 400 letters to publishing houses. I followed up with phone calls. Basically, everyone said no, we don't buy this, our staff people do it. We don't need it. And then everyone had an emergency. Everybody assured me that this was one unique emergency and that there would be no more business. They all became steady clients. I've worked for everybody again except one client. That's how I got in the door."

Public-relations free-lancer Sally Chapralis had her own way of finding clients when she started: "I called all the people I could think of in the field, starting with all my former employers' competitors. I began there, not as any retaliation to my employers, but because I assumed that the competitors would feel that I specifically had something to offer them. I sold myself, and it worked. I also used the grapevine to find out about possible clients whenever I felt comfortable doing so. Mostly, though, apart from the initial calls I just described, I went in cold."

When you are looking for clients, or even for a special area in which you might sell your services, here are some places to conduct your search:

- Public library. They will have lots of vocational information, and you may uncover some special area you had not considered.

- Your local chamber of commerce. They can tell what is going on in your community, where demand is greatest and lowest. This works especially well in a small community.

- Universities, particularly ones where you have studied. One free-lance librarian got his start by simply mentioning his intention to free-lance to the dean of his school. That was three years ago when he was completing work on a master's, and the dean is still diligently referring clients to him.

- City and state government agencies. Like the chamber of commerce, they can help you find your niche based on your community's specific needs.

- Field offices of the Small Business Administration. Most offices have retired executives, members of the Service Corps of Retired Executives (SCORE), who will be eager to help you in your new venture. Call your regional office.

- The U.S. Department of Commerce. They don't have anything like SCORE, but they do have an interest in supplying you with information about any areas that you may be investigating for their free-lance potential.

- Field directories and guides. They are too numerous to list here, but just to give you an idea of what is available, here are a few possibilities. In advertising, *The Creative Black Book* is the "telephone" directory, so to speak, of the business; in publishing, people use *Literary Market Place*; museum workers refer to the *International Directory of the Arts* or the *American Art Directory*; librarians use the *American Library Directory*. There are also any number of annual handbooks and periodicals that provide information about and sources of free-lance work. R.N. *Magazine* for nurses advertises hospitals' personnel needs throughout each issue, and they also publish an enlarged edition that is an annual review of nursing positions. Writers can choose from the sources listed in *Writer's Handbook*, *Writer's Yearbook*, and *Writer's Market*. Comparable books are published for commercial artists, designers, and photographers. In addition, books published to guide you through your specialized field may offer advice and ideas on finding clients. In photography, free-lancers (and others) turn to *Selling Your Photography: The Complete Marketing, Business, and Legal Guide* by Arie Kopelman and Tad Crawford (New York: St. Martin's, 1980); commercial artists and designers use *Selling Your Graphic Design and Illustrations* by Tad Crawford and Arie Kopelman (New York: St. Martin's, 1981); authors who want to learn the ropes of getting published use *How to Get Happily Published: A Complete and Candid Guide* by Nancy Evans and Judith Appelbaum (New York: New American Library, 1982).

   Most libraries have a copy of the *Foundation Directory*, which contains information about more than 2,500 foundations; it is a useful tool for anyone else who plans to solicit work or grant money from them. The list for all free-lance careers is too specialized to cover here, but explain your needs to a librarian, and don't be surprised when she or he produces a book that lists potential clients. It's that simple. If you can afford to buy the book, it may be a worthwhile investment. Sometimes, as with *Literary Market Place*, published by Bowker, you can order the book from the publisher; at other times, you may have to join a professional organization to get a directory. The point is to find the books, annual special issues of magazines, periodicals, guides, and directories that apply to your business. Ask others who do the kind of work you do, and check with your local librarian. Regardless of how specialized your area is, there are guides and directories that will help you.

- Your colleagues. Most free-lancers will not pass along their active clients, but they will share inactive clients or general leads ("Call Bill Smith; I hear he needs free-lancers now.") with someone who is just starting out. Also use this as an opportunity to find out what it is like to work for various clients. Free-lancers love to share this kind of information and will be very honest with you.

- Catalogs and sales sheets. If possible get this information from prospective clients, from the chamber of commerce, the library, or by calling the clients, if that is feasible. This way, you can really pinpoint the kinds of services a client is likely to need.

- Your own survey. This takes a little nerve. Call up potential clients and ask them if they ever use free-lancers. Jack Sharp, a free-lance typesetter who was looking for areas into which he could expand his business, decided that employee handbooks were a possibility. He further decided that small manufacturing companies might be a prime target; they were too small to have advertising agencies who would do this work for them and were large enough to need employee handbooks. Most were union operations, too, another reason they would be interested in publishing a guide to employee relations and benefits. He called twenty small manufacturers and found out that five were definitely interested, twelve had no interest at all, and three wanted to talk more about it. Those numbers represented a high level

for Research writing - etc.)

of interest to Sharp, who only wanted to handle four or five of these projects a year to supplement his other free-lance typesetting. For him, a survey resulted in sales.

LETTING CLIENTS FIND YOU

As your free-lance practice builds, clients will begin to come to you, and you can look forward to making fewer and fewer calls to prospective clients when you do not have a name you can use to get you in the door. Ursula Beldon, a successful set designer who has never worked any way but free-lance, said she eased into this situation right after school, although she acknowledged that going to the right school in her field helped immensely: "I made contacts at Yale and got my first assistant's job before I graduated. It's all word-of-mouth in my business. You do one job for someone who likes your work, and they recommend you to someone else."

A free-lance indexer said, "Now I occasionally get jobs where my name has come up third-hand. Someone I worked for told someone else, who in turn, without knowing me, passed my name on to yet another person. I used to start looking for new work as soon as I was finishing a job. In the last year I haven't had to do much looking on my own."

One therapist in private practice recalled, "I have one client who was recommended by the sister of an ex-client. That sister lives in London, and she gave the name to someone who was coming back to the United States. Then I have what I call my great-grandchildren among clients—friends of friends of friends, or third-generation clients."

Never hesitate to develop a network of people—friends, acquaintances, colleagues—who can refer clients to you. You should do this in a low-key manner, though, but keep in mind that people like to help others. If your work is good, which it must be anyway for you to survive, then friends and acquaintances will be delighted to recommend you to prospective clients. One person whose free-lance business consists entirely in ghostwriting books for others noted, "Referrals are the only way I get work." Robyn Cones, a free-lance masseuse, has no choice but to build her business entirely on referrals. She notes, "My business is all by referral. I can't advertise because of the nature of my business. I tried it just once and got too many loonies."

Joining Professional Organizations

There are several things you can do to ensure that clients will find you. The most obvious is to join professional organizations and groups where you will meet others who may need your services. Often these groups publish directories of their members, and anytime you can get yourself listed in a directory, you are liable to pick up some extra business. But directories will probably be only a small portion of the business you will receive through your professional activities. For the most part, just mingling with other group members will be enough to build your business.

Speaking of the kinds of contacts he builds through professional associations, free-lance librarian Bryan Johnson commented: "Solicitations for free-lance work are very informal, and you often don't even realize you've been offered the job until you've already been interviewed—say, at a professional meeting or even at a social gathering. You need to project an image of self-confidence all the time. You have to believe in yourself. I'm never obvious at a professional meeting. I keep a high profile, though. I always mention to people that I free-lance. I often find that people are more interested in my free-lance work than in my regular job."

The first step, then, is to join any and every professional group or organization that could possibly be a source of clients or client referrals. Don't however, join a group without first considering what it can and cannot do for you. It is important not to waste time on a group that isn't right on the mark in terms of what it can do for you professionally. Sometimes this is easier said than done—finding just the right group takes effort. Michael Tucker, a free-lance business consultant, remained a member of a group of professional builders because his last employer had been a contractor and he had always belonged to that particular group. Eventually he took stock of his situation and realized that he had gotten very little business from the group and that in fact most of his business came from architectural firms. He began attending meetings of a group of professionals who worked in architecture, and soon was getting more referrals than he could handle.

Whenever you are thinking of joining a group for professional reasons, consider the following:

- The number of members. Is the group large enough to be a viable source of contacts for you?

- Who the officers are. Are they real movers and shakers in your field? If so, that is a good sign.

- The benefits offered by the group. While Zimmerman was going to become less active in the free-lance editors' group, she did buy group insurance through them, so she had no intention of dropping her membership. The reverse is also true for free-lancers: You may want to join a group with which you have only tenuous professional connections because they provide a benefit you badly want and can't get elsewhere.

- The yearly dues. Some professional groups are prohibitively expensive to those who are just starting out. Don't join if you really can't afford the dues; you'll only resent the membership later.

- What the group has accomplished. You should only join groups that are highly respected by the persons who hire the people in the group. Associating yourself with a group that has a reputation for being flaky or disorganized won't help build professional contacts.

Professional Subscriptions

In addition to joining groups, subscribe to and read your profession's trade publications. Their advertisements can be an excellent source of free-lance contacts, and they also enable you to keep your eye on developments within the profession. Trade magazines also provide information about movement within the profession, sales and mergers, new acquisitions, and trade shows where you might contact new prospective clients.

MAKING THE INITIAL CALL

As you go about the treacherous business of selling yourself, remember that the very first calls you make are the hardest. And to be totally honest, it is a very rare free-lancer who actually enjoys soliciting work. There are two kinds of calls: cold calls and calls where you do, in fact, have a connection, however tenuous it may be. Most initial calls are made by telephone.

The value of having a connection may be overrated, as many free-lancers have discovered. You personally may obtain a feeling of legitimacy when you have a name to use as you make a call, but its real value has yet to be proven. And consider this: If you are diligent about making cold calls, following up with a letter and then yet another phone call, you may find that you have achieved the same kind of rapport by the third or fourth contact that you would have if you had a connection.

Set designer Ursula Beldon offered proof that making cold calls frequently does pay off: "If you don't have the right contacts in the theater, but your work is really good, you can sometimes get through to designers for assistant's work by calling on them to show them your portfolio. I got my present assistant that way. He sent me a résumé in the mail, and I needed someone, so I met with him and liked him and hired him. It wasn't all that smooth—actually, he had kept in touch with me through several phone calls. But I was a cold call on his part."

A free-lance business consultant says, "I write or call people out of the blue. I don't mind writing letters, but I hate making phone calls. I've learned, though, that if I'm not successful right away, often I hear from people ten months later. It works out in the long run, but I don't like the phone work. It makes me feel awkward. It helps to know that I'll get some work. It makes it all seem less futile."

One free-lance writer offered this hint on getting yourself motivated enough to make cold calls, or for that matter, any kind of sales calls: "I try to set aside one morning a week when I know I have to build up my business. I usually pick Friday morning. I do it because I plan a reward for myself when I'm done. Sometimes I have a nice lunch with a friend. If I have the time, I go to a movie or even take the entire afternoon off."

When making initial sales calls, either by phone or in person, remember that first impressions count for a lot. If your phone personality is abrupt or unpleasant or if you don't present yourself well in person, then you are less likely to get a job than is the free-lancer who takes care to make a good first impression.

Initial calls are important, whether they occur by phone or in person. If you are nervous about your ability to carry things off, practice what you are going to say or role-play with a friend to make sure you present yourself well. There is little else you can do except to be yourself and be as relaxed as possible. Try to avoid putting on a formal voice or a manner if you can. Keep small talk to a minimum especially on the phone. Because you are home all day, you may find yourself in a chattier mood than usual when you do call someone; remember, though, that the person at the other end is in an office and won't find idle chitchat pleasant.

Speak in your most pleasant voice. Don't interrupt the person you talk with, but be prepared to end a long awkward silence, perhaps by asking some questions about the kind of work the company does or about some detail of their work. Act enthusiastic; remember you initiated this entire process, so you are the primary person who wants something. A little enthusiasm goes a long way when you are soliciting business, but don't brag; if anything, err on the side of humility. But if you are asked to describe your work experience, which you almost surely will be, then be specific about what you have done even if you don't want to name clients. If at all possible, float the names of a couple of your major clients in front of the person whom you are talking to. Prospective clients are often reassured to know that some big names have hired you. One enterprising free-lancer always claimed a major airline as one of his past clients, although he had been subcontracted through another free-lancer to do some work for the airline and never worked directly with them.

Records of Your Calls

As you make calls—cold or otherwise—and as you call on people, you will need some record of this activity. One free-lancer reported on her method of keeping track of whom she had called and what had been discussed: "I keep a small file box with three-by-five-inch index cards. On one side of the card, I write the vital statistics—company name, address, name, and title of person I have to talk to, kind of work I might do for them, who suggested I call, and so on. On the other side I note the date of the call and what we discussed. I don't write much, but what I write is very meaningful. Because I only check in with someone every month to six weeks and I may never have met them, I note when I called and the exact date when I'm supposed to call back. If we happened to discuss anything personal, I make a note of that. For example, one person I work with is crazy about cats, so I have a note to that effect. Another person is an aspiring opera singer in her free time, so I have a note about that. These notes help me place the person, and if the occasion does arise for a little small talk, I have a hint of what to talk about." A free-lance artist's representative has a similar system, and she also adds small brightly colored metal clips to her cards, coded to the week or month when she wants to make a follow-up call. A photographer's representative carries a small notebook that contains an index card for each advertising agency, where it is located, and what work his photographers have done for it in the past.

Another free-lancer who had worked for a highly organized man acquired his habit of keeping a detailed log of all phone calls. She said it paid off the only time she had to threaten to sue someone. She had put in several hours on a project, which the client had later canceled and then had refused to pay her for the work she had done. Her ability to cite details of their dealings, including his verbal commitment to her, caused him to render payment rather than risk a legal suit. Few free-lancers ever have to sue for their money, but many free-lancers work on a casual basis that does not include contracts or confirming letters, so keeping a phone log is an excellent idea.

Regardless of how you make your initial contact, the purpose is to obtain some business or to build a solid enough relationship so that you will be called in for future assignments. Successful contact has been made when your skills and talents match the needs of your prospective client. Sometimes you just get a lucky break, as one young aspiring costume designer did. After weeks of calling an established costume designer about the possibility of working as an assistant, he finally connected with the woman on a Saturday afternoon. She told him she was working in a theater and could meet with him briefly there. He headed over, sat down, and chatted with the woman for a few minutes until she said, "Well, when can you start?" Thinking that he was being very eager, Jackson replied, "How about Monday morning?" The designer one-upped him, however, by saying, "How about right now?" He became a costume designer's assistant that afternoon. This free-lancer admits that he had laid his groundwork for his lucky break, having previously sent samples of his work and having diligently called the designer back every single time he was told to do so. He does attribute their finally connecting for what turned out to be a long and happy association to his luck in thinking to pick up the phone on one particular Saturday afternoon, when he thought he just might catch the designer in her studio at a relatively quiet time.

Part of making contacts requires knowing when to give up. Sometimes someone just does not have any business for you and never will, but never comes right out and says it. Sometimes, as photographer's representative Barbara Lee learned, you just have to have a second sense about when to quit. She commented: "I have no special technique for getting through to a prospective client. There's no courtesy on their side. They never call me back. I just keep calling until I get hold of them. Either they're busy, or they're away from their desks, and there are plenty of $200 a week secretaries and receptionists who don't want me to make a living. I do have some sense that anyone who has treated me really badly won't want to see my face again. If someone stood me up, for example, I just drop it. I now can feel where I'm going to get work and where I'm not. I know where to push and where not to push. I'm very persistent, but there is a time to call it quits."

FREE-LANCERS' RÉSUMÉS

The subject of making contacts also brings us to the subject of free-lancers' résumés. There will be occasions when you will be asked for a résumé.

A free-lancer's résumé should never run more than one or, at most, two pages. Ideally, try to get everything on one page. Put your title—Writer, Editor, Typesetter, Set Designer, Actor—at the top of the résumé. A sample of a free-lance editor's résumé is on page 132. Because there are so many areas in which people free-lance, it is impossible to print representative sample résumés, but the one that follows shows how to describe your free-lance business. In some professions, such as acting, set designing, or dancing, a résumé is unnecessary, but in many fields it can serve as a sales tool—subtle advertising, as it were.

JOHN DOE, III
EDITOR/REWRITER

481 West Barry Street   Telephone: 312-657-8670
Chicago, Illinois 60657

Areas of Specialization

Social sciences, particularly political science and psychology; business; adult education. Secondary and college levels.

Experience

I have worked on all levels of textbooks and have a strong production background. My editorial and production skills include developmental work, writing and rewriting, and copy-editing. Am also experienced in public-relations writing.

Clients

McGraw-Hill	Bols (Brown Foreman Distillers)
St. Martin's	Simon & Schuster
M. Evans	Graphic Alliance, Inc.

Employment History

April 1978 to present: Over six years ago I began my own editorial services business, supplying various clients with a variety of production and editorial services.

October 1973 to April 1976: Project editor, Madsen Textbook Publishers, Inc. Worked in social sciences and adult education.

October 1970 to October 1973: Senior editor, Flynn Publications Worked in social science.

June 1968 to October 1970: Associate editor, Flynn Publications

Education

B.A., Iowa University, 1968, education

THAT ALL-IMPORTANT
APPOINTMENT

After all your work in establishing contacts, you will eventually get some appointments to see people who can offer you work. An appointment is important, something that you should prepare for carefully. The rules for a free-lance appointment are much like those for a job interview, which after all is exactly what this is. Here are some pointers:

- Dress appropriately. That means wear something comparable to what you expect to find the person who interviews you wearing. Later, when you are working for someone, you can pop in and out of the office dressed more casually, but for a first call, dress like a professional.

- Take samples of your work if possible.

- Show that you have done some homework on the company by your ability to talk intelligently about their needs and how they might put you to use.

- Be prompt for the appointment. You may be kept waiting, but you should always be on time.

- Be prepared to meet several people. If the person you meet with likes you, he or she may want you to meet others in the company. Always go to an appointment prepared to meet more people than the one with whom you have set up an appointment.

- Ask what specific jobs are coming up and find out whether or not you will be considered for them. Be a little brazen about presenting yourself as the person for the job. This is not the same as bragging. Rather, it is the age-old technique of closing the sale. If you don't say, "Well, that certainly sounds like an interesting project, and I would very much like to handle it for you," that may be the only reason you don't handle it. Ask for what you want—the worst that will happen is you will be told no. And that kind of no is hardly a permanent no; it merely means that you are not considered right for this particular job or that it has already been promised to someone else.

- Finally, one woman discussed one more aspect of the free-lance interview that was echoed by many other freelancers. It has to do with a kind of tension that often exists between those who live the free-lance life and those who do not. She noted, "I try not to appear too successful when I call on someone. There's a free-lance mentality about that. I think that sometimes the people I work for would like to do what I do, but they're not secure enough to do it or they're afraid to do it, so they don't want to know or think that the grass is greener on the other side, so to speak. They don't want to know that I can afford to go to Europe or California."

LEAVING ROOM FOR REPEAT BUSINESS

Once you have made your calls, had an appointment, and finally gotten an assignment and completed it, the next phase of handling your contacts is follow-up. Handling this stage can be tricky, and your technique will vary from business to business. One thing tends to apply to all freelancers, though: You often have to follow up, or you may not be called again. Yet, even if a company is eager to use your services and uses you almost constantly for several months or even a year or longer, the day will come when the work will slack off. It doesn't mean you won't ever get any more work from this client; it just means you are in a period of "staying in touch." How regularly you stay in touch and the means you use depend on your personality and that of your clients. For everyone, though, the trick is to keep your finger on the pulse of your client's operations without becoming a pest. This may mean a weekly call; it may mean a monthly call. It may not mean a call at all but might require a letter.

Follow-up is a very low-pressure kind of sales work. A good guideline is that as soon as you get any concrete information about when a client will next have work for you, jot it down on your notecard or whatever you use, and then don't call back until it is time to check on that specific assignment. Tell the client you will call a couple of weeks before that date to check on the assignment so he or she knows that you have not vanished. You no longer have to waste your time on phone calls, nor will the client dread the morning mail or the ringing of the phone because it might be a particular free-lancer for whom he has no work at the moment.

Once you start getting repeat business, your life will be immeasurably easier, and your self-confidence will soar. One longtime free-lancer said this is exactly when he solicits new business. "I always make calls for new work when I'm busy with present work. For one thing, I think I look more desirable if I say that I'm busy at the moment, but I just wanted to introduce myself and let them know that I'm available. I think clients talk more freely about future projects because they know I'm not desperate for work. But mostly it's good for my ego. It doesn't hurt at all and can even be fun to call prospective customers when you're feeling good about yourself because you've got a full in-basket."

When those repeat business calls and letters do start, here are a few guidelines for responding.

By Phone

1. Answer your phone promptly. If you have a phone machine, make sure it answers right away and instruct your answering service to respond by the third ring when you are out.

2. Say "hello" or your name. It's a little ostentatious to use a company name, even if you have one.

3. Write down the substance of all phone calls. You will get many assignments over the phone; the phone log is a good record to have.

4. If you have more than one line or call waiting, dispense

with additional phone calls quickly and very politely. Don't ask people to hold but rather, say that you will call them back right away.

5. If you need to look up some information, ask the person waiting if he wants to hold on the line or have you call back. If you know you cannot put your finger on the information right away, then say you will have to get back to the caller.

By Letter

1. Your letters should sound businesslike and friendly, not chatty.

2. There should be no typing errors.

3. Indicate your intentions clearly in the letter. Never beat around the bush.

4. Put as much as possible in writing without offending a client or making him think you do not trust him. Remember you need not confirm by letter in a formal way; you can just drop someone a line in which you happen to mention the assignment, its fee, and due date.

GETTING ALONG WITH CLIENTS, AND VICE VERSA

There is an art to getting along with clients. On the one hand, free-lancing offers many opportunities for making new friends, and free-lancers often become friends with the people they work for. After all, there is no employee-boss relationship here, so that barrier does not stand in the way of friendship. Many persons who hire free-lancers said that they like to become friends with the people who work for them. As one person said, "It helps to become friends with the people you work with. I try to. The more you can communicate to the people about what you want, the better and easier it is for everybody. I don't have to give orders. Everything happens on a very pleasant basis in which I ask questions and supply answers, and vice versa. It's a very cooperative venture."

There is a negative aspect to the looseness of the free-lancer-client relationship. At least until you learn to establish some authority, you may be walked over by certain clients. One successful free-lance editor said, "Many editors, even senior ones, act as messengers. And they don't charge for it. I sometimes deliver the finished product to meet the editor, but I don't act as a messenger. I make my connections, but once I've made them, unless we both need to talk with the manuscript in our laps, I don't pick up projects. Editors do, all over town. It shocks me. You get treated as you behave, and this is one of those little things that is very important. When someone asks me to do something I don't consider professional, I say, 'Gee, I wish I could do that.' That's a nice phrase to remember.'

Another free-lancer reported, "People try to waste my time. They want me to come in and talk before they've shown me the work. I always say, 'I can't tell you anything until I've seen the project.' Sometimes someone refuses to mail or messenger originals, so then I say, 'Fine, I'll come down in a cab and charge you for it and for my time.' They usually quit right then. What they're really angling for is to save a messenger fee, and once they learn they can't do it, they start behaving."

Working in Someone Else's Office

Perhaps the hardest thing to juggle is on-the-premises work in an employer's office. Few people reported resentment from the staff over their freedom to come and go and keep the hours they pleased, but many said the lines of authority were not always as clear as they might be. When this confusion arises, the free-lancer can initiate the conversation to clear up what work is expected and who will give out assignments. Sally

Chapralis noted, "When I have worked in other people's offices, it has been my experience that when I am actually on the payroll, as opposed to free-lancing out of their offices, then my status is lower. I am regarded as a part-time employee, so to speak, and although I have had some authority and status, it wasn't as much as I had when I have free-lanced. This kind of limbo is not as psychologically rewarding as having my full independence as a free-lancer or being a full-time employee. It is up to the free-lancer to establish that mood and her status immediately. If you do that, you won't have any problems working in someone else's office." Bryan Johnson does most of his library work in other people's libraries, and he reported that he had to learn to establish his authority in order not to waste time: "I'm much better now than when I started. At first, I tended to be too grateful, almost groveling. Now I'm not terrible about it. I don't barge in and start rearranging furniture, but I let clients know in a fairly strong way that I will need a typewriter and a desk or workspace. I make sure they know they have to provide these for me. I don't go in like gangbusters, but I don't act mousy either. If they didn't want the work done, they wouldn't have hired me. If they want it done right, I need these things. I rarely have trouble now that I've learned to be stronger about these things."

LETTING SOMEONE ELSE SELL YOU

If all else fails, and you really hate selling yourself and do not do a good job of it, then think about hiring someone to sell you. Persons who sell the services of others are called agents or representatives, which is usually shortened to "rep." There are two times when you can quite legitimately get an agent: (1) when it is the custom in your trade, as it is with almost all authors and with many photographers and artists, and (2) when you can't face selling yourself.

The one hitch is that there are some trades where you simply would be laughed out the door if you had a personal representative. Free-lance editing is one such profession. On the other hand, you can always band together with several other editors and let someone represent all of you; that would be tolerated, if not greeted with open arms. As you can see, even if agents are not the custom in your profession, there are often ways around this. And if you are in a business where agents are the rule, then you are foolish to go without one.

In almost all free-lance professions where agents are the custom, the agent or rep takes 10 to 30 percent, depending upon the field and the kind of arrangement that is standard. To get a reading on the going rate, ask other people who do what you do what they pay their agents.

When looking for an agent, try to find someone who has the following traits:

- Good business sense. After all, this is the part of your work that you are hiring him or her to handle.

- Sense of organization. Again, if you can't stand this part of the job, get someone who is good at it.

- Handles others who are like you. For example, a large agency is not the place for a beginning author, however much you may be seduced by its reputation. Get someone who will pay personal attention to you. This applies in every field where agents are used.

- Good sense of follow-up. A good agent is always one step ahead of his clients. He calls you about prospective work or a bill that is due to you before you have a chance to call him.

The very best way to get an agent—perhaps the only way—is through word-of-mouth referrals. Once you have the name of someone who might represent you, arrange a meeting if possible. In sizing up an agent, trust your instincts. This person will know a great deal about you financially, and your earnings will be based in large part on his or her ability to sell. If you like him, chances are that other people will, too.

Finally, here are some pointers on getting along with an agent:

- Get a contract, if that is customary in your field, spelling out what each of you owes the other. Some fields, such as music and publishing, are exceptions. Musicians do not sign with an agent, even though he may be working for them, until a third party has offered a contract. At that point the musicians and agent draw up a contract with each other. Between literary agents and authors, there is also often no contract, although increasingly today agents are asking their clients to sign letters of agreement.

- Find out the etiquette of your business and follow it. An author's money, for example, always goes to his or her agent; that is a sign of friendly relations between the two. These are the little things you need to know when you start working with someone.

- Keep your agent posted on your business dealings. For example, if you run into some prospective business at a party, inform your agent. Don't make any deals without your agent—he is there to negotiate for you. Remember— that is why you hired him. Never undermine your agent by negotiating on your own. The best way to avoid ever being in this situation is to say, whenever the subject of money or contracts comes up, "You'll have to talk to my agent about that."

- Give your agent any information, sales tips, or pointers that will help him sell you, but spare him details he does not need. Most successful agents are busy people; therefore, any information you can give him about how to sell your services will help him. One writer said she always considered her attempts to help her agent successful when she sat in an editor's office and heard him describe the sales potential of her book in the same words that she had spoken earlier to her agent. Your agent, on the other hand, does not need to hear how difficult a time you are having researching something or exactly why you need fast payment for a finished project.

- Settle your agent's fee, and then forget it. Your agent, strictly speaking, is an independent entrepreneur just as you are. He does not work for you as your employee. He will, if he is any good, work very hard on your behalf and completely earn his commission, so it is only good manners to be gracious and thankful to this colleague and not to begrudge him what you pay him.

- If things are not going well between you and your agent, talk to him about it and possibly end the relationship. Never gossip about your agent to others, especially people in the same business. Word of your dissatisfaction might get back to your agent and make him or her work less hard for you. If you are unhappy with your agent, fire him or her *before* you hire a new agent.

All About
Fees

7

You have probably already accepted the fact that you are not free-lancing to get very rich. All things considered, though, you cannot afford not to give serious thought to how you set and maintain fees—and to a regular, systematic review of your fees. Free-lancers need to recognize that while they may not get rich, with astute handling of a fee schedule, there is no reason they cannot live quite well. Too many free-lancers earn less than they might because they do not push for as much money as they are worth, nor do they negotiate as well as they handle the services they deliver. One free-lance dog walker, a veteran of fifteen years at this kind of work, who could easily command 30 to 40 percent higher rates than he does, started low and has never raised his prices much. He is, by his own admission, "simply too timid to look someone in the eye and demand a substantial increase."

FIGURING OUT WHAT
TO CHARGE

The hardest part of developing a fee schedule is figuring out what to charge. Free-lance fees in all fields are rather idiosyncratic. Rarely can a free-lancer set an across-the-board price for services. Most free-lancers, like it or not, have sliding fees. Some old, favored clients are always charged less than newer, more affluent clients. Some clients are charged overtime and for rush jobs, while others never are. And in almost every field free-lancers charge different rates for corporate or commercial work as opposed to creative or literary work. A set designer reports that he does television commercials only because they pay so much more than his theater work. He noted, "I can use one successful commercial, on which I earn royalties, to subsidize two off-Broadway shows each year. I want to do the off-Broadway shows because people in theater see my work, and because it's creative. I don't get as much satisfaction from the commercial work, but I do get paid well."

Then, too, there are various ways to structure a free-lance fee. In the course of one year a free-lancer is likely to take on jobs that pay by the hour, the day, and by flat fee. Those who work in publishing have even more ways to charge: by the page, by the line, by the number of rewrites.

What does it all mean to someone starting out in free-lancing who is unsure what to charge or even how to figure out a fee schedule? Basically, a free-lancer should not get too caught up in working for one preset fee—for example, for one hourly rate. Sometimes a client will pay you less per hour, but you can pad the bill (some managing editors, for example, routinely tell free-lance editors to do this) so you end up earning as much as you would if you charged a higher hourly rate. Sometimes you take a commercial or consulting job that is not particularly interesting or challenging but which pays well, so you can later take on creative work that does not pay so well. The trick is to charge enough overall so that you earn what you need to earn. But even a sliding scale or a willingness to negotiate does not mean that you will not require a well-planned rate schedule. If you ever go into a meeting to settle a fee and are unsure what to charge or what you would like to earn, then you will probably walk away a loser. You must always be prepared to negotiate, and you should expect to earn what you are worth 90 percent of the time. To do this, you need to figure out in advance what the general fee ranges will be for your services. The only danger is in setting an hourly fee and measuring all your work by that one standard.

One independent literary agent discussed the dangers in thinking only of what your time is worth hourly when you work for yourself. He said, "Some agents tell me that they won't spend much time looking over a contract for $2,000 on which they are only going to earn $200 because they figure their time is worth X amount per hour, and they simply cannot afford to do this. I take the opposite view. Of course, I would always prefer to work on a $10,000 or $50,000 or $100,000 book contract where I may earn $1,000 for one hour's work, but I also figure that since I earn that $1,000 for one hour, then I can afford to earn $2 an hour on another contract. That's where it becomes difficult, if not impossible, to establish an hourly rate for some kinds of free-lance work." A writer who writes under his own name for various publishers and also does a considerable amount of ghostwriting took a similar view: "I always gain more satisfaction out of my own writing, the stuff to which I attach my name, than I do from the ghosting jobs, but the ghosting jobs pay more. Let's say I earn $25 a page when I ghost. No publisher has yet paid that much per page when I write under my own name. But I figure I use the ghosting to support my own publishing endeavors—which will someday, I hope, pay me more."

Overpricing Versus Underpricing

When setting your fees, you must take care that you neither under- nor overprice yourself. Both spell disaster. If you underprice, you will always be trying to make ends meet, never earning as much as you could and possibly never earning enough to make a go of free-lancing. You are also less valued, most free-lancers feel, if you work cheap. Sharon Neely, who has recently become successful enough to turn down work, thinks doing so has been good for her business overall. She noted, "I can afford to charge my new clients more than I charge my old ones because I am turning down business. At first it scared me to turn down business, but I quickly got into the swing of it. Then I saw the connection between that and what I charged. Even as a beginner I resented working for some clients who did not pay well, and my goal always was to weed out those people. I think my rates have always been somewhat high. My instincts tell me that it impresses the people I work for. They think because they are paying more, they are getting more, the same way that they are more eager to hire me and will call me back right away when I'm too busy to take work. My work is good—I think they are getting more."

Another free-lancer reports, "I often raise my rates during recessions. I get more work because publishers tend to fire staff and use free-lancers more. It's cheaper for them. When money is tight for a client, though, it is tight for me, so that's when I ask for higher rates. Inflation hits everyone."

If underpricing won't let you earn a healthy living, neither will overpricing, which may be an even greater danger in free-lancing since no one may tell you this is the reason you aren't getting any work. If you overprice, you lose work to persons as qualified or even less qualified than you are who charge less. You also won't get repeat business.

Getting a Fix on the Going Rate

Figuring out what to charge, not only when you are just starting out but also when you have been free-lancing for a few years, is rough, mostly because of the many variables discussed earlier in the chapter. Ideally, setting rates should be easy. You should be able to calculate your overhead (rent, equipment and supplies, insurance, and so on), and then divide by the number of jobs you expect to get during the year. The result is the rate you must charge per job. Reality is something else again.

The first thing you must do is discover what the going rate is in your field. There are two basic ways to do this: One is by comparing notes with colleagues, who are usually more than happy to discuss their rate-setting woes with anyone who will listen, and the second method is to check with clients. Clients, in fact, often will tell you what their rates are. If not, you can always ask. One free-lancer, investigating a new specialty, called potential clients to ask what they normally paid. You should also check professional organizations and directories that may provide information on the going rate.

Finally, before setting your rate, you should take your overhead into account or at least know what it is. An example of how to do this follows:

Overhead	Monthly Cost	*8·83*
Rent	$120	*$120.*
Equipment and supplies	$180	*$50.*
Utilities	$80	*$25.*
Insurance	$48	*$35.*
Accounting and legal fees	$25	*$100. car*
Promotion	$50	*$100.*
Salary (what you pay yourself)	$2,000	*$1,000.*
TOTAL	$2,503	*$1,430.*

If you calculate your monthly costs this way, remember to include only business expenses; for example, the $120 sum for rent represents one-third of the monthly rent for a free-lancer who works out of his home and spends $360 a month on rent. If this free-lancer averages four jobs per month, then he

$357. per job at
4⟌1430.   4 jobs
*   12   per month*
*   23*

must be paid an average of $625 per job in order to meet his overhead. Calculating overhead is a good technique for a new free-lancer and even for a seasoned hand who wants to double-check his rate structure. It is not the entire picture, though. Setting free-lance rates always calls for an extraordinary measure of flexibility. Clearly, you have to set rates that will provide you with a comfortable living by your own personal standards, but you must also take into account your competition, what the market will bear, and the fact that a very wide-ranging rate scale may still be the best way to achieve your objectives.

NEGOTIATING FEES

To negotiate well, you need a lot of self-confidence. You have to appreciate what your services are worth (a lot!) and be able to convince someone else of that. What you do not have to do that scares many people is think quickly on your feet. When most free-lancers think of negotiating, they often conjure up images of a smoke-filled room where tough guys sit around with cigars in their mouths and the strongest man browbeats the others into accepting his view. Or they picture the tough corporate executive who always knows instantly what is the right thing to do. That, fortunately, is not what negotiating is all about—or at least the level of negotiating that free-lancers do. In free-lance negotiating, you not only can, but you must, use your own personal style. And usually, perseverance always goes a lot further than toughness.

If you have done your homework and considered your fee carefully before setting it, then most of the time the fee you ask for will be accepted without question. When someone does decide to negotiate with you, these negotiations will be based on your fee. Set your fee fairly high when you think you will have to negotiate, but keep it at market value, taking your experience and the going rate into account. Consider, for example, the difference in negotiations when you ask for $10 and when you ask for $20. If $10 is over budget, the client may try to reduce your fee to $8. He would never attempt to reduce it to $8, on the other hand, if your asking price is $20 per hour. It may come down to $18 or $15, which is still double the $8 fee.

One good thing about free-lance negotiations is that you never again have to negotiate against your present salary, as you often do when looking for a job. On the other hand, you will never get the substantial increases in your free-lance fee that you could get from a major boost in salary. For that reason, you must be sure to set your fee high enough before you begin negotiations.

The next rule of free-lance negotiation is never to quote a fee or price off the top of your head. Always insist that you need time to think this over. Ask to see some of the work you will be doing or a proposal of what will be expected of you. In almost every field, there is something you can see that will help you size up what the work is worth. Wherever possible, be sure to get your hands on this, whether it is part of a manuscript to be edited, an outline for a book, a musical score that needs a lyricist, an unproduced play that needs a director, or a play that needs a set.

Finally, although this may seem minor, when you are going to negotiate fees with someone, dress well. People form instant impressions of one another, whether you like it or not. And if you walk into a negotiating session in messy or inappropriate clothes, the other person will immediately take your measure—and possibly decide that money does not matter to you. If you are sized up as someone who does not expect very much, not very much is exactly what you will get.

When you begin to talk money, there are a few things to do to help your cause. Name your price first. The first person who mentions price has an edge in that he has more or less set the range of the negotiations. If someone wants to pay you $1,500 for a job, and you had $3,000 in mind, then you will have difficulty mentioning the $3,000 once the ballpark figure of $1,500 has been mentioned. By the same token, if the potential client has $1,500 in mind and really wants you to do the work (which he presumably does, if you have reached the stage of discussing money), then several things are likely to happen when you mention $3,000. The person may realize that his figure of $1,500 is unrealistically low for this type of job. You may go up a notch or two in the potential client's judgment, and he may revise his figure upward accordingly. Or the person may tell you quite honestly that this is more than he had hoped to pay, but he will see what he can do about meeting your fee or coming closer to it. Keep in mind that if your fee has been set at a reasonable figure, on a par with what other free-lancers in your field charge, then there is no reason for a potential client to get you for less—very much less, that is.

On the other hand, do stay open to some level of negotiating. Sometimes you can trade off a reduced fee for something else. For example, if you ask for $3,000 and settle for $2,000, that may not be unreasonable if more work is forthcoming. If this happens, explain that you will lower this fee one time, on the condition that if the client likes your work, he will be willing to pay your full fee the next time. Usually, he will. Or if there are two projects, you might lower your fee if you are assigned both at the same time—in writing. If you don't want to open negotiations with one hard, cold figure, then mention a range within which you would be willing to work. When you do this, the high should be fairly high because you will undoubtedly settle for less. The low end of the scale should never be any lower than you are willing to work for.

Here are some additional hints on negotiating freelance fees:

- Don't accept the first offer. If you ask for $10 and are offered $8, quickly come back with $9.

- Don't use personal needs as a reason why you should be paid a certain fee. No one cares if you have alimony to pay or need a more expensive apartment.

- Be aware of your worth; you may have to defend it (more on that later).

- Concentrate on selling your strengths, not your weaknesses.

That makes you worth more. Never talk about what you can't do or haven't done if you can help it. Either say you're sure you could learn something quickly or that while you cannot do A, you are very good at doing B.

- Don't talk money until you are sure the person wants to hire you. Before someone knows he wants you to work for him, a high fee could make you look less desirable. After someone definitely wants to hire you, he or she will be eager to work out something amenable to you both. This is even more true for free-lance employees than for full-time ones. A company that has a pay scale and simply cannot hire you at a certain price may pay you more than that to work free-lance, which brings us to a touchy point: defending your worth.

Occasionally, someone may be crass enough to point out to you that your free-lance fee is higher than the salary paid to a full-time employee who does the same kind of work you do. Your response should be, "That's true, but the total cost of getting the work done is less. You don't have to provide me with benefits, vacations, social security, and you don't have to pay a bookkeeper to keep track of all that."

You also may find that the announcement of your fee is greeted with something like, "But that is more than we usually pay free-lancers." There are two possible responses to this: "I'm worth it," and "Then start me low and give a raise on the next assignment if you like my work." If that doesn't close out the conversation, you might add, "This job is a lot of responsibility and work, and I want the pay to be commensurate."

Once the fee has been set, be sure to jot it down somewhere. Illusions of glory in the heady aftermath of successful negotiations have been known to strike free-lancers and cause them to remember fees as being slightly or even greatly higher than they actually were.

The Question of Overtime

Free-lancers rarely can charge overtime for their work since they do the work entirely on their own time. If you choose not to work from 9:00 A.M. to 5:00 P.M. when the rest of the world works and want to charge extra for working 5:00 P.M. to 2:00 A.M., you will not have a chance. Alternately, if you claim that you will have to work long or excessive hours on a project, it is not likely to carry much weight with a client, who will probably pull part of the project and give it to someone else. There is one time, however, when you can justify charging overtime, and that is when a client calls you for a rush job or to work over a weekend or on a holiday. If a client wants a job done too quickly for your taste but in a reasonable amount of time, charging overtime will not work, but if a client wants a job done in a very big and somewhat unreasonable rush, in such a way so that you clearly would have to work overtime on evenings and weekends, then you can say you will charge extra. Alternately, you can raise your hourly rate or add a percentage surcharge, whichever you and the client agree to. If the client is truly in need of your services, this is one time when he will probably gladly pay them.

Charging Expenses to Clients

You must also decide whether or not to bill your clients for expenses such as messenger services, copying, postage, telephone bills, and other similar items.

If you bill the client for miscellaneous expenses and are reimbursed, then you cannot deduct these expenses. On the other hand, if expenses run high, and your funds are tight, you may have no choice but to bill for expenses.

Free-lancers bill them in one of two ways: They either add them in a clearly itemized fashion to the invoice they submit, or they bury them in the bill. One free-lancer who uses a messenger to pick up work, for example, usually adds an hour or two to the cost of the job. Even free-lancers who do their own pickups and deliveries often charge for this service by adding their time to the bill.

Package Prices

Occasionally someone will ask you to set a per-job, or flat fee, price; or, depending upon your field, this may be the only way you set your fees.

A package price, as per-job prices or flat fees are often called, is nothing to worry about if you know how to calculate it. If you don't, it is an excellent way to lose money. First, never quote a package price unless the work is clear-cut and limited. Free-lance librarian Bryan Johnson never accepts a package price, for, as he says, "I work hourly because people tend to find still more work for me while I'm working on one project. If I had established a package price, I might get caught." Sally Chapralis, whose stint as a public-relations free-lancer led to many different kinds of assignments, noted, "Unlike straight editing where I could charge an hourly fee, the public-relations work didn't lend itself to that. Even when I work in someone's office at an hourly fee, I often end up doing projects such as newsletters or brochures that I would have charged more for had I been working for an hourly fee. Generally, for a brochure or report or presentation, I offer a package price that includes one rough workup and one final copy of the work; anything beyond that gets billed at an hourly rate." Her method is good for people in public relations, advertising, commercial art, and other areas where the limits of an assignment are difficult to define.

In calculating a package price, figure out exactly how many hours you will spend on a project, add in all your expenses, and then add about 10 percent to be sure you are covered. If you can't project the number of hours that will be needed, follow this suggestion from Sharon Neely: "I edit a few pages until I find my pace on a project. After that, it is easy to know exactly how many hours I will need to complete a project." When you submit a package price—before you do the work—send a letter stating what the fee will be and exactly what it will cover. Note that any additional work will be billed at the regular hourly rate. Clients will have no qualms about asking you to do rewrites or fix something in some other way if you have accepted a package price, so be sure to state clearly how much "fixing" you will do for the project.

No project should include an unlimited amount of repair work, particularly if it results from a client simply changing his mind about what is needed. If you sense that you have a client like this on your hands, decline to work for a package price. Often if a client wants the package price only so he can take advantage of you, he will probably back off from the package price when he realizes that this is not going to be possible.

Sometimes free-lancers establish a flat fee that is negotiable if they end up doing more work than was originally intended. A negotiable flat fee is generally bad business practice for a couple of reasons. First, if you set a fee and then decide that you really need to charge more midway through a project, you may end up looking unprofessional—or worse, like a whiner. You should be able to establish a fee at the outset of a project and stick to it. If you cannot do this, do not work for a flat fee. Second, although a negotiable flat fee is often based on whether or not you are asked to do extra work, you and your client may not see eye-to-eye on what is extra work. What you consider a major overhaul, he may claim is minor reworking. If there are likely to be gray areas such as this, your best bet is to decline to work for a package price at all.

WORKING ON SPECULATION OR CONSIGNMENT

Especially as a new free-lancer, you will occasionally be asked to work on speculation ("spec") or on consignment. When you work on speculation, you write or produce something for no pay and submit it to someone you hope will buy it. Usually, the potential client has expressed an interest in your work, but there is no firm commitment to buy. When you work on consignment, you place a work with a seller who is basically an intermediary, such as an art gallery owner, and you get paid when the work sells. Some free-lancers—artists, for example—have no choice but to work on consignment; most other professionals will not work on speculation.

The advantages of working on spec or consignment are as follows:

- Your work is seen by persons who might not see it otherwise.

- You have a greater chance of selling something than if you refuse to work on spec or consignment.

- This may be the only way to get started, especially if you lack contacts or are switching fields.

The argument in favor of working on spec or consignment can be summarized by saying that you have nothing to lose. If you have no choice but to work this way, and this usually refers to consignment more than to spec work, then by all means go ahead. You cannot buck the trade custom and will only cut yourself off from important sources of income. For free-lance writers and others in similar fields who are often asked to work on spec, it is better by far to avoid this if at all possible. Consider these disadvantages to spec and consignment work:

- You get no money until your work produces sales, if on consignment, or until the work is accepted, if on spec. The buyer is essentially under no more pressure to buy your work than if you had never discussed a spec assignment and had simply sent your completed work in unannounced and unknown.

- The money you spend on an assignment is tied up until you sell the work—and then, the money may be slow coming in. Work sold on consignment often does not reap any financial rewards until months after the sale; persons who work on spec often are not paid very quickly, either. Free-lancers, unfortunately, often are at the bottom of a long list of suppliers to be paid, but this is especially true with spec work and work done on consignment.

- It is not professional. One writer worked out an excellent response to anyone who asked her to write on spec, as new clients occasionally did despite her experience. She always said, very sweetly, "I would love to do that, but I write for a living, so I can't afford to do any spec work." Free-lancers beware: More than once you may have to remind someone that free-lancing is your only source of income. And if it is, then you cannot stay afloat working on speculation or consignment.

The offer to work on spec may only be a bluff. One writer with impeccable credentials but new to a particular magazine was told that they only hired new writers on spec. She offered her regrets and said she never worked that way. The editor and writer parted company amicably, and about four hours later the same editor who could only hire new writers on spec called back with a fat assignment. Another writer who had recently switched from public relations to writing articles about beauty was asked to work on spec. At first she was inclined to accept, since the editor's argument that she was switching fields seemed to make sense. She was smart enough to say she would have to think it over since she normally did not write on spec. Unwilling to confront the editor on the phone, she wrote a note saying that she could not work on spec but would do the article for $400, which was half her fee. The editor accepted her offer as if there had never been any discussion of working on speculation. Moral: Even if you feel you have no choice but to do some work on spec or consignment, always try to bluff your way out of it first. And as soon as you have enough clout not to work this way, don't. The only way to get out of working on speculation is to say no. The way to lessen the hazards of working on consignment is to ask for a draw or insist on payment within a certain amount of time after a sale is made. Once you have established a reputation, these are not hard things to negotiate.

Don't write on spec!

THE QUESTION OF CREDIT

Most free-lancers are too small to be able to extend credit to their customers. Their cash flow is not smooth enough; they can't afford to give up the time needed to collect on overdue monies; and they usually don't dare spend the money before they have collected it. Most free-lancers are aware of this, though, and never consciously extend credit to anyone. Surprisingly, though, many free-lancers extend credit without realizing it. You extend credit any time a customer owes you money and doesn't pay you. That customer is getting an interest-free loan from you. In effect, free-lancers extend credit by letting bills go too long and by not collecting promptly on overdue bills. Usually, too, when you find yourself in this situation, you are likely to have a deadbeat on your hand, which means that you must take immediate action.

You should always have a deadline for when you consider a bill overdue, and when that deadline arrives, you should do something to get your money. One of the ground rules of free-lancing is that the person who makes the biggest fuss is often the one who gets paid the fastest. One free-lance commercial artist reported this story about his first job, which was for a major airline. He knew they were good for the money, and he was surprised when it didn't arrive promptly. After thirty days—his limit for payment of a bill—he went to the airline's central office and started complaining. Since the airline was a huge corporation, people were surprised at his personal touch, and while eager to pay him, no one seemed to know quite how to go about getting him his money. He bounced from manager to manager, carried forms, showed copies of his invoice, until he finally got a check that was specially drawn for him—after being told that this was impossible. He also never had to go through that again. He believes it was because the airline knew he would become a pest if not paid promptly. And yes, he continued to work for the airline through many happy years.

Dunning on Overdue Bills

The minute a bill is overdue—whether you decide that is after ten, twenty, or thirty days is up to you—send a second invoice. In capital letters, type SECOND INVOICE on it. The next step is to call the person who hired you to remind him or her that you have not yet been paid. Sometimes you can do this under the guise of checking to see how he liked your work, and just incidentally mention that you haven't been paid yet. If your client shows dismay and promises to attend to the situation, you probably will be paid right away.

Different free-lancers use different techniques at the next stage. If you haven't heard within ten or fifteen days, then you must do something else. One sure way not to be paid on time is to get a reputation as someone who never follows up on such matters. This is one time when being a pest works in your favor. One free-lance editor reports: "I keep bugging the editor who hired me. I figure it is her responsibility to nag accounting until I'm paid." Another free-lancer said, "I go over the client's head to accounting. Nine times out of ten the client never even knows I've called accounting. I'm very nice—say I'm just checking on my bill. I always get the name of the person in accounting, and I make sure he or she knows my name. I never let the person call me back; I always insist on calling back myself. I usually get paid right away. And after I've tracked down my money this way several times, the people in accounting catch on, and I get paid promptly." She added, "There's another advantage to going directly to accounting aside from the fact that they get to know you, and that is that you often learn when checks are issued. For example, if you submitted an invoice the last week in a month, and you know the company pays on the first and the fifteenth, then you know enough to call them right after the fifteenth if you haven't been paid."

Another free-lancer who goes directly to accounting warns: "You can usually do this only with large companies. I often work for individuals who own the company. I would never go over this person's head to his accounting department."

After your second invoice and several phone calls have been ignored, it is time to write an official letter, one that reiterates what has happened, states the amount you are owed, and indicates that this is the last formal warning. It is not worth your time to hire a lawyer to do this, but if you have a good friend who happens to be a lawyer, then his letterhead might carry more weight than yours.

There are, of course, some other ways to entice your client into paying, and while they are not so hard-line as an official letter, they are also less likely to get results. You may, however, wish to try them, particularly with longstanding clients. First, consider charging interest on bills not paid promptly. To do this add a statement to your invoice indicating that you will charge interest if the bill is not paid in a certain number of days. Then on the second invoice, add the interest charges. In all honesty few free-lancers try this, and the interest is rarely collected by those who do, but some free-lancers feel this helps them to get paid promptly. What is more likely to be effective is to offer a discount for early payment. One free-lancer tried this when a bill was one month overdue and found that he was promptly paid. There is only one problem with this: It is not particularly businesslike. Still, it is a desperation tactic that may work.

When you call someone about an overdue bill, don't hesitate to trade on being a small business, as free-lance organizer Stephanie Winston did with a major New York corporation that did not pay her promptly. She said: "I called a vice-president and said, 'Listen, I'm a small vendor,' and then I got my check right away. I allow about thirty days before I start agitating. I call the person who hired me; I send a second invoice." Admitting that you are small is also a subtle reminder that your bill probably isn't that large, either, and therefore not that hard to pay.

Always maintain close contact with anyone who owes you money. Silence from you may cause your creditor to think you have gone away or given up. On the other hand, don't make any threats that you do not intend to carry through.

Once an account is seriously in arrears and after you have sent at least one invoice and a letter, you can do one of two things: (1) turn the matter over to a lawyer or collections agency, or (2) file in small claims court. Either gesture often has a magic touch. One free-lancer told of a client who arbitrarily refused to pay because the project had been canceled, something, she noted, "that did not change the fact that I had done my work on the project, and I expected to be paid. I said I would sue, and I did. We settled out of court for about half of the bill."

Few free-lancers have to sue, and those who did often settled out of court. Since you won't want to run up a large legal bill, it may be a better use of your time and money to settle out of court if you possibly can.

Almost every state has a small claims court where you can file for a small fee, describe your case to a judge or other arbiter, and get an immediate decision. You need not take a lawyer into small claims court, and the person you sue cannot take one to court with him. There are monetary limits in most small claims courts; they vary from about $150 to $3,000, depending upon the state.

If you have a legal problem and little money, it is worthwhile to try to find free or inexpensive legal services. Free legal counseling is occasionally offered by professional groups. Artists and writers, for example, can turn to Volunteer Lawyers for the Arts, a group organized to provide free legal help to those whose incomes do not exceed $7,500. If your legal problem is minor, consider using a legal clinic or storefront legal service even though the lawyer you see may not specialize in your specific field. If your problem is more complicated, you should seek the advice of the best legal specialist you can afford, even if you can only afford one meeting with him or her.

Once you are paid, note this in writing, or you may feel the acute embarrassment of one free-lancer who called to complain about a bill that had actually been paid: "I consulted for a company, so they paid me a monthly fee. They were a little sleazy, though, and that combined with my overeagerness to be paid meant that I called them one day in my toughest voice and asked where my check was. I had received it a week earlier and simply hadn't carefully noted what month it was for."

Before you cash a check, always examine it carefully. Is it made out to you? Is it for the right amount? Even more important, look for any kind of disclaimer or waiver of your rights. More than one writer has blithely cashed a check only to later discover that by endorsing it he had sold all rights to his work.

The majority of free-lancers cannot report a single incident of not having been paid, but all can report times when they had to go right down to the wire to get their money. One free-lancer said, "I've had one stiffed bill. Eventually, I was told by the client that he was going to cut down the bill. Someone later told me that this particular company does that when they have budget problems. I also worked directly with someone I didn't like who also didn't like me. The production editor accused me of not getting clearance on one quote. She said she had put in three days on it. I asked what she found out, and she admitted she learned the quote was in the public domain. I said that's why I hadn't cleared it. I suggested that, in the future, she should always call me first if she had a question. It went on and on, exchanging letters. After seven months, I said very simply, 'Pay me or I'll see you in court.' They paid me."

Creditors also have several tricks they can employ when they want to slow up payment, so having a check in your hands doesn't always mean that you have been paid. Watch out for:

Unsigned checks
Checks so sloppily written that you can't cash them
Partial payment with "Payment in full of all obligations" written on the back
Someone who stops payment, claiming that an error has been made

When You Suspect Your Client May Not Be Able to Pay

Occasionally, you will have a client whom you do not totally trust for one reason or another. He may personally be upright but may work for a company that operates on a shoestring. Or he may be what one free-lance ghostwriter calls a "private" client—someone who has no affiliation with a corporation who wants to pay a ghost writer out of his personal funds to write something for him. Good businesspeople usually develop a sixth sense for whether or not someone will be good for the money. Unfortunately, many free-lancers cannot afford to turn down such business or are reluctant to do so for various reasons, not the least of which is that it often pays quite well. What, if anything, can you do to increase your chances of timely payment when you suspect someone is a deadbeat? Actually, there are several things you can do. Many free-lancers ask for an advance from such a person. Barbara Zimmerman said when she does copyright searches for individuals, as opposed to publishers, she always asks for an advance. She noted, "The one time when I forgot to do it, they didn't pay me."

In addition to getting an advance, you can ask to be paid as you turn in segments of work or complete certain aspects of the project.

If you suspect that someone will not be able to pay, definitely put all arrangements in writing. If possible, write something in the letter of agreement or contract that protects your rights should you not be paid. Ghostwriters, for example, often include a clause in a letter of agreement stating that the work belongs to them until they are paid.

RAISING YOUR FEES

On a more cheerful note than nonpayers, consider that the day will come when you will need to or want to raise your fees. Most free-lancers do this sooner or later, although many do it rather casually. Judy Waggoner, free-lance typist and copy editor, said: "I do not raise rates regularly, but rather, I have a sliding scale, which I adjust to the status of the client (publishing houses are better equipped to pay than are struggling authors!). I also adjust to the difficulty of the assignment. I try to keep a feel for what the market is paying and keep my rates competitive with that." Zimmerman said, "I raise rates in two ways. First, I just raise them. Then I have rush and nonrush rates. Rush rates apply when I do work quickly or work on weekends. I quote the higher rate to new clients. I generally raise the clients I think will be amenable, and when I have raised most of those, then I raise the ones I may lose. One huge client with a once-a-year project said over lunch, 'No rate raises.' I'm going to have to deal with that, but I'm waiting until I'm in a better position to negotiate that one. They're a large portion of my business, so I'm not raising them now."

Masseuse Robyn Cones has yet another method: "I usually raise a few people who are new. Then I give two-months notice to my regular clients. So far, I've never lost anyone, and my rates have almost doubled since I started. If someone has sent me a lot of business, I will give a free massage. Most people are willing to pay more, which always amazes me, but then I'm still inexpensive compared to what other masseuses charge."

There aren't many guidelines to setting new rates, but the following may help you handle this potentially explosive situation:

- Tell new clients first.

- Raise old clients only after you have developed new clients at the new rate.

- Be as tactful as possible when you raise rates. You need not apologize, but you can sound contrite and rather sad that you have to do this.

- Be prepared to lose some clients.

Finally, do review your rates regularly. Other workers get raises, and there is no reason that free-lancers should be denied this reward for work well done.

Putting It in
Writing
8

Two very good friends—and free-lance colleagues in the writing business—were having a festive lunch to celebrate having decided to work together on a project that neither one had time to handle on a full-time basis. They were going to write a newsletter for a corporate client. The writer who sold the newsletter would serve as primary liaison with the client; the other writer would do the bulk of the research; then each writer would alternate taking charge of the bimonthly publication. If all went well, they had dreams of expansion; there was even the lucrative possibility of a newsletter they would write and own themselves. That, they both felt, was where the real money was; meanwhile, this was an excellent way to test the waters, both in terms of their ability to work together and in terms of finding out whether they liked writing newsletters.

Only one sour note marred the happy occasion, when one writer pulled out a three-page letter of agreement outlining their shared and separate responsibilities and the financial split. He handed it to his partner, adding, somewhat apologetically, "Look, if you were my mother, I would still insist that we draw up a letter of agreement, so here is one for you to look over. I think of this as a way of protecting not only our business relationship, but also our personal relationship."

The partner balked, saying that he could not understand why a written agreement was necessary among friends. Eventually, though, both partners signed, and they have, despite occasional differences, enjoyed a long, mostly harmonious—and certainly clear-cut—relationship, personally and professionally. Not only does this fable have a happy ending—not always the case in fables—but it has a moral that all free-lancers should heed, which is: Put everything you possibly can in writing, and be suspicious of anyone who does not want to commit himself or herself to signing an agreement.

In the case of these two writers, reluctance to sign the letter of agreement genuinely was based on a common but misplaced fear that too heavy or formal a dose of business arrangements can ruin a friendship. Actually, as any free-lancer, or for that matter, any businessperson who has ever worked with friends or acquaintances can report, the opposite is true. Settling the business arrangement in as professional a way as possible only strengthens the bonds of friendship, not vice versa.

Of course, arguments do arise, but these arguments would come up sooner or later, anyway. They are more readily settled if there is something in writing that defines the relationship. If the arrangements are clear-cut from the beginning and in writing, there is a lot less to quarrel about.

When someone who is not your friend shows reluctance to put your agreements in writing, be leery. Ask yourself why. Does this person anticipate that he will not be able to make good on his part of the arrangement, and is he or she looking for a possible way out should this be the case? At the very lowest level, you must consider that this person may be trying to cheat you in some way.

Occasionally, someone will resist putting something in writing because that just isn't the way he does things, or because that isn't the way things are done in your field. This is still no reason for you not to put your agreements in writing.

Brace yourself, weather the laughter or derision or whatever you are subjected to for being so businesslike, and then continue to insist on a written agreement. The fact that so much of what free-lancers do is casual or handled by spoken agreements is all the more reason to make every possible attempt to firm things up as much as you can.

Putting things in writing does not necessarily mean that they must be drawn up and presented as formal documents. Casual free-lance agreements, such as when a copyeditor is assigned a manuscript by a managing editor, do not call for either a contract or a formal letter of agreement. A simple confirming note will do, in that case, indicating your acceptance of the assignment and the date the work is due, as well as the money you will be owed. The following is an example of a friendly confirming letter:

Dear Jack:

This is just a note to let you know that I received the manuscript today, and will begin work on it first thing tomorrow morning. I'll have it back to you on the twentieth, in return for which I shall submit a bill for $10 per hour for my work. I've edited a few pages, and I think that your estimation that no more than seventy hours will be required is accurate, as usual.

Perhaps we can have lunch when I turn in the work. I'll talk to you, in any event, as work progresses.

Cordially,
Marie

As you can see, legal language is not called for; first names will even suffice. What matters here and in any "official" correspondence you write as a free-lancer is that the relevant "facts" or conditions of the agreement are set forth.

THE LEGAL DOCUMENTS OF FREE-LANCING

You don't need any special forms to prepare any of the documents that free-lancers normally write. Invoices, letters of agreement, and contracts can all be written on your own letterhead. Many people who hire free-lancers on a regular basis said they would consider a preprinted invoice or contract slightly officious anyway.

What follows is advice on writing—or reading—the most common documents that free-lancers must deal with.

INVOICES

In order to be paid, you should write and submit an invoice. Always keep carbons of invoices, so you will have a quick reference of what you are owed and the date when you billed the job. An invoice should include the following information:

1. The date

2. Your name and address

3. Your social security number

4. The name and address of the person for whom you worked

5. Description of the project and number of hours worked

6. Statement telling whether invoice is for full or partial payment

7. Amount of money you are owed

8. Terms, or when due, plus any discounts for early payment or announcement of your intention to charge interest

Some invoices in which various types of billing are shown can be seen on pages 167–69.

Submitting the Invoice

Depending on the kind of work they do, free-lancers have a variety of ways of submitting invoices. Most people submit their bills with the finished project, although if the project is long, they bill monthly or at several points throughout the project. One free-lancer noted, "I always send an invoice because it is more professional. Occasionally, a client gives me an invoice form to fill out, and I will do that. Mostly, though, I prefer to submit invoices on my letterhead. I also mail them a day or two after I complete a project. That way, when I have worked on several projects during the month, I can do my billing all at once."

Bryan Johnson gives his private library clients an invoice as he leaves a job. He added, "I'm thinking of having a letterhead printed so I don't have to keep typing my name and address at the top of every sheet. It looks more professional."

INVOICE

May 1, 1982

TO: Henry Smith
45 East Fourth Street
New York, New York 10009

FROM: Jane Jackson
1300 Michigan Avenue
Chicago, Illinois 60600

Family Therapy
20 hours consulting @ $30 per hour $600

NOTE: 10 percent discount for payment remitted within ten days.

Jane Smith
123½ West Ninety-eighth Street
New York, New York 10025

INVOICE

May 1, 1982

TO: John Doe, Publishers, Inc.
20 Oak Street
Chicago, Illinois 60611

Editing and rewriting chapters 1, 3, 5, 6, and 8 of
Family Therapy ms.
60 hours at $10 per hour (partial bill) $600

Thank you. Please remit within twenty days.

Stephanie Winston, who organizes for private and corporate clients, says, "I walk up to my clients at the end of a day and hand them a bill with a smile. They always pay me right then. Corporate clients are different; I submit invoices to them and get paid later."

Sometimes a client will have an invoicing form that you are expected to use. One free-lancer, who resented these forms because they made her feel like a child, commented, "They also mess up my bookkeeping. I type all my copies of invoices on pink carbons, so they are easy to spot. The employer's

---

INVOICE

DATE: May 1, 1982

TO: John Doe, Producer
Downtown East Theater
45 E. Fourth Street
New York, New York 10009

FROM: Jane Smith
123½ West Ninety-eighth Street
New York, New York 10025

Set design of *Doing It Right*

(preliminary sketches, model set,
supervision of building of set) $3,000

---

forms are white, and they don't look like my invoices. So I submit their invoices, along with my own typed invoice. Sometimes I don't send them an extra copy, but I always make one for myself."

Whether you use a client's form for an invoice or type your own, never let anyone else write your invoice. One inexperienced free-lancer forgot to write an invoice when he turned over an assignment. The client pressured him for one and offered to type it up on the spot, which the free-lancer allowed. Later, when the check arrived in the mail, it was less than the free-lancer thought he was owed. When he called the client, he learned that accounting had caught a discrepancy between the total amount and the hours worked. The client had to take the invoice to his boss a second time for approval.

By the time the free-lancer called, the invoice had been on the boss's desk twice. The client was unwilling to take the invoice to his boss a third time, so while both agreed the money was owed to the free-lancer, who had, in fact, not given the correct number of hours to match the total charged, the client suggested that the free-lancer make up the loss on the next assignment. There was nothing the free-lancer could do but agree. The money would obviously be forthcoming, but not for several weeks. Of course, if the free-lancer made a fuss, he would have gotten the money sooner, but doing so might have jeopardized his chances of getting that next assignment. Besides, both the client and the free-lancer were partly at fault in this situation. And a somewhat sticky situation that, in effect, did cost the free-lancer money, could have been avoided had the free-lancer written his own invoice.

Most free-lancers like the idea of breaking up a large bill, if only for psychological reasons. One person noted, "I bill midway through a project and at the end. For a big project I bill four or five times. I found out that the size of the bills boggled people's minds, and they handled small bills more easily. Small bills also help my cash flow, so now I bill once a month even if the bill is small."

Another astute free-lancer commented, "I also pay attention to the round figures on an invoice. If my hourly rate works out to a total of $1,000 for example, I may decide to bill $980 because it looks like much less than $1,000."

LETTERS OF AGREEMENT

Wherever possible, write your own letters of agreement. The other party may change them, but at least you have started on your terms. As noted earlier, letters of agreement need not be formal. One free-lancer described her system for writing letters of agreement, adding, "I never feel more businesslike than when I am drawing up a letter of agreement. First, I go through my old file of letters of agreement to see if there is one I can modify to this situation. I always keep letters of agreement. The first one I ever wrote was modeled after one my agent had written for me and another writer, and I think I've essentially been revising that one ever since. I write out a list of the things I want to cover. Then I put the list aside. When I look at it again, the next day or even a few hours later, I often think of something to add. Finally, I write up the letter of agreement. I use first names if the letter is with someone I know well, but I make sure it looks official. I always type in lines where the signatures are to go, for example." (See sample letter of agreement below.)

Another free-lancer reports on a method he employs for putting things in writing when he senses resistance to a written form: "I write a confirming letter in which I restate everything we have agreed to verbally—the price, the deadline, the amount of work I will do for the price." A word of warning: Since this kind of letter is not signed by both parties to the agreement, it does not carry the weight of either a letter of agreement or a contract. On the other hand, should questions arise later concerning the nature of the work, the letter still is better than having only a verbal agreement. Several samples of informal confirming letters follow.

LINDBERG-ELMER Letter of Agreement

October 11, 1982

Frances Lindberg   Patricia Elmer
414 West 91st Street   527 West 98th Street
New York, New York 10025   New York, New York 10025

Dear Patricia:

Our signatures at the bottom of this letter of agreement will signify our acceptance of the terms described herein regarding the preparations for the manuscript tentatively titled *Nutrition*, due to be delivered on December 1, 1982, to Fred Jones.

1. Frances will deliver to Patricia all notes and other work pertaining

to manuscript, along with an outline of content of each chapter.

2. Patricia will use these materials to write a manuscript of approximately 75,000 words.

3. Frances will edit Patricia's work, and if rewriting is required, Patricia shall undertake it upon receiving specific, written directions from Frances.

4. Expenses incurred during the preparation of this manuscript, such as copying and typing, shall be shared equally between Frances and Patricia.

5. Should Frances undertake the writing of individual chapters, Patricia's fee will be reduced by $125 per chapter, and that sum shall be paid to Frances.

6. All monies to be paid for this project shall be rendered by Daniel O'Neill, literary agent, to Frances, less agent's fee, who shall in turn be responsible for rendering the following flat fee to Patricia: $2,340.

7. If Patricia fails to produce a manuscript satisfactory to Frances within the time agreed, Frances may, at her option, terminate this agreement. In the event of such a termination, Patricia shall retain all sums received by her and shall forfeit all further interest in the work, and shall return to Frances all materials related to the book.

ACCEPTED   _____

                    Patricia Elmer

                    _____

                    Frances Lindberg

DATE_____

ALLISON-STROMBERG Contract

January 23, 1983

James Allison   Joe Stromberg
5749 Fairfield   4212 Olive Street
Chicago, Illinois 60659   Elgin, Illinois 60120

Dear Jim:

This letter summarizes the agreement that the two of us have entered as of this date, whereby I shall develop and submit to you a proposal for revising the workload structure of your fabric-manufacturing plant. The terms of the agreement are as follows:

1. You shall instruct your appropriate department heads to open all records to me that relate to the operations of the plant and its workers.

2. I am obligated to work under strictest confidentiality regarding any information I obtain related to the operations of your plant.

3. Within eight weeks I shall submit to you in writing a proposal for plant reorganization. The report shall include details of function as well as of cost.

4. Within three weeks you will review the project and meet with me to discuss those suggestions that are immediately applicable. After this meeting I shall submit a revised report within three weeks of those suggestions requiring further work.

5. The terms of payment are as follows: $4,200 payable as follows: half on signature of this letter, one-fourth on completion of initial report, and one-fourth on completion of final, revised report.

Please sign all copies of this letter. Keep one for your files, and return one copy to me for my files.

cont.

Accepted and agreed to by:

_____   _____
James Allison   Joe Stromberg

WITNESSED BY: _____

DATE: _____

Here is a checklist of things to consider including in any letter of agreement, informal or formal:

1. Complete names and addresses of both parties

2. The date of the letter of agreement, which can appear at the top or bottom of the letter or contract.

3. Brief description of project, including dates when work is to be turned over and amounts of monies owed.

4. Who owns the work or services you provide (if applicable to your field). When writers do "work for hire," for example, that work is usually owned by the person who commissions it. The creator of the work relinquishes all rights to future income and may not even have any control over how the work is used or whether it is used if this is written in the contract. Always check the back of any check given to you in payment for any work you do to make sure that you are not relinquishing rights you do not intend to waive by signing the check.

5. Places for all parties to sign and a line for a witness, if necessary. A witness is necessary if the letter or contract is liable to be questioned. Anyone can witness the signatures, or you can have a notary witness them. Witnesses, which are very important in wills, for which the primary signatory will not be around to confirm his signature, are far less important in the kinds of contracts free-lancers draw up.

In any letter of agreement, try to cover every possible situation: what you are responsible for, what the other party or parties are responsible for, who will owe whom what amount of money, when the money is to be tendered, what specific materials or supplies that one party is to supply to another, and what will happen in the event that the project does not work out. In the letter below, which is between a writer who is ghosting a book and a celebrity whose name will appear on the book, the ghostwriter keeps any money she has been paid at the time if the agreement falls apart, but she is obliged to return all materials related to work she has done to date.

GLENN-McGUIRE Letter of Agreement

March 25, 1983

Dear Margaret:

Our signatures at the bottom of this letter of agreement will signify our acceptance of the terms described herein regarding the preparations for the manuscript tentatively titled _____
_____, due to be delivered on _____
to _____.

1. Margaret will deliver to Carol all necessary research, outlines, notes, and other work pertaining to the manuscript, as outlined in the proposal.

2. Carol will use the materials, adding new material and original writing, to prepare a manuscript of approximately _____ words.

cont.

3. Margaret agrees to assume typing expenses related to preparation of the manuscript. All other expenses will be shared equally between Carol and Margaret.

4. Margaret instructs Daniel O'Neill, literary agent, via this letter to pay Carol 60 percent of all advances, less agency commissions, paid to her by above publisher, and 50 percent of all subsequent earnings, less agency commissions, of the work.

5. If Carol fails to produce a manuscript satisfactory to Margaret within the time agreed, Margaret may, at her option, terminate this agreement. In the event of such a termination, Carol shall retain all sums received by her and shall forfeit all further right, title, or interest in the work and shall return all materials furnished to her by Margaret.

ACCEPTED

_____

Margaret Glenn

_____

Carol McGuire

_____

WITNESSED

_____

DATE

Written Documents for Work on Speculation and Consignment

If all else fails and you do accept an assignment on speculation or you must work on consignment, then be sure to draw up a contract or letter of agreement (or write a confirming letter) delineating the terms. It should include the following:

1. The exact amount you will be paid if the work is sold/ accepted.

2. Who has loss for responsibility. When artwork, for example, is placed in a gallery on consignment, it is usually the artist who bears the responsibility if it is lost or damaged, but often you can get a gallery to share this responsibility with you. You should always try to do so.

3. The conditions for storage and display. Be very specific here so you will have a case for yourself if you have to establish who is responsible for damages.

4. The period of time work can be displayed; if work is done on speculation, then note period of time during which work must be accepted. After that you can pull your work and show it elsewhere.

5. When you will be paid. If a gallery sells your work for a sizable sum, but agrees to time payments, are they obligated to pay you when the sale is made or do you receive your fee in lump sums as they are paid? Also, the letter of agreement or contract should note whether you find it acceptable to have your work paid for over time. If you are a writer or artist working on spec, note when you are to be paid. This could be when you turn in an acceptable work or when the work is published. A few magazines pay on publication, and to those that do, if your reputation is big enough, you can probably write a letter that arranges for you to be paid on acceptance.

6. Especially if you work on spec, you should ask for reimbursement for expenses. Again, this should be put in writing.

When people do work on spec or consignment they often make the mistake of assuming that there is nothing to put in writing. As this list shows, this is clearly not the case.

CONTRACTS

Most free-lancers occasionally have to deal with contracts, which are nothing more than a more detailed version of a letter of agreement. Sometimes a business will change so that where contracts were not normally used, they now will be. Due to changes in the copyright law, this has happened with magazine writers. The law now states that the author has full ownership of articles and that the magazine must negotiate everything after first serial or first publication rights. Formerly, magazines often bought all rights from writers—occasionally even by devious means such as a disclaimer on the back of a check or simply because the writer failed to note what rights he or she was selling on the invoice. Now because writers do not automatically relinquish their rights, publishers have become interested in contracts and letters of agreement with writers. Whenever the business shifts toward putting agreements in writing, free-lancers should rejoice.

But even if a contract comes in and it does not suit you, always question anything that you do not like. Occasionally, the other party will settle one issue with you but still not write the contract to your liking. This happened to two coauthors whose publisher wanted to own the option on the next book they wrote together as well as any books they wrote separately. It was decided that the publisher could have an option on their next book together but no more than that, since they both had other writing commitments. When the contract appeared on their agent's desk, the option clause, which everyone assumed was settled, contained yet another surprise: The authors were supposed to supply a finished manuscript for the next book. When the authors and their agent got done fixing the contract to their satisfaction, the troublesome option clause read only that they must submit their next proposal for a joint book to the publisher. The publisher's lawyers had obviously tried to wring out the best deal they possibly could, but had the authors and their agent not been astute in reading the contract, they might have signed away far more than they intended. Even if contracts are fairly standard in your business, as they are in most businesses, never assume that the contract you receive is, in fact, standard. Always read it carefully; always check it carefully and never hesitate to question anything you think is perhaps not in your best interest. It probably isn't, and it probably can be fixed.

Here are a few things to consider when confronted with a contract:

- Treat every contract, including a preprinted one, as an unfinished document. Too many people think a contract is final simply because it is in print. You can and should query anything that does not appear to be in your best interest or to your liking. Most clients, in fact, expect you to raise questions and to negotiate the *fine points* of a contract.

- Check the contract to be sure it contains the basic information in correct form: your name, address or domicile, property under discussion, date due, adequate description of work, amount to be paid, when it will be paid.

- When negotiating a contract, that is, before you get the final copy, settle on special matters such as your expenses or the kill fee that is to be paid if the work you do is not actually used. Be sure ownership of the work that results from your services is clarified.

A Note About Agents and Contracts

Too often, a free-lancer with a good agent (or representative), or even a free-lancer with a not-very-good agent, thinks that he or she no longer has to look at contracts before signing them. Nothing could be further from the truth. You should never sign anything, no matter how well represented you have been, without reading it first. Furthermore, a good rule of thumb for contracts negotiated by an agent is: The less money involved, the more carefully you should read the contract yourself. Only a rare agent does not devote a great deal of time and effort to a high-paying contract; many agents give less than full attention to the smaller ones, so it behooves you especially to check everything carefully on your small contracts.

Dealing with fees and legal documents is for many free-lancers the least interesting part of their business, although a few free-lancers do become increasingly involved in such dealings. One well-known artist disdained the very idea of discussing such matters when he started out, but quickly learned that he had to know how that part of his life functioned if he wanted it to run smoothly. He reported, "I really believe that many of the artists who make it big, so to speak, do so because they run their lives in a professional, businesslike manner. I reluctantly decided to pay attention to these things. I think of these activities as something to do on a slow work day. And it doesn't interfere with my creativity one bit."

Settling Down to Work

9

A major concern of free-lancers—beginners and seasoned ones—is how to manage time wisely. Some free-lancers worry about working too hard, and free-lancing has been known to bring out the workaholic in many people. Others worry that they will lack the discipline required to structure their days. They fear that without a boss or other authority figure looking over their shoulder, they simply won't produce. Ironically, both problems plague all free-lancers from time to time; free-lancing seems to be the kind of work where you can be a workaholic one month and then feel totally burned out the next. The time and efficiency sacrificed to these problems, however, can be kept to a minimum if you make an effort to manage your time well.

The workaholism may be necessary to get a free-lance business off the ground or to ease anxiety over starting a business. It is most often a problem for those who work at home, where the work seems always to be staring you in the face. Most free-lancers, though, go through a period of being excessively involved with their work and then taper off. A typical attitude is that of Sharon Neely, who said, "After two years, I'm starting not to work on weekends. I'm feeling more secure and making more money with my editing, so I don't feel the financial need to work weekends." Margaret Stein, also a free-lance editor and rewriter, took longer to realize that she need not be such a slave to her business. She said, "For years, especially during my busy season in summer, I worked late practically every night and right through most weekends. I was even earning enough money so I didn't have to do that. It was just my busy season, and I didn't seem to be able to shake the notion that I should kill myself for three or four months out of every year. Finally, I took a summer house out of town. It seems that my concern for money, which had propelled me to work so hard during the summers, now propelled me toward the house every weekend. I couldn't stand not to use the house since I had paid for it. Anyway, it broke the pattern."

As for worries about not having the self-discipline needed to free-lance, those who don't simply do not survive very long. Beyond learning how to manage your time, successful free-lancing requires a heavy dose of certain personality traits such as discipline, concentration, and the ability to keep the world at bay when necessary.

MANAGING YOUR TIME

When you work for someone, your time is often structured for you. When you work for yourself, you and you alone are responsible for how you spend your time. There are three things to be concerned with when considering how you spend your working hours: (1) how you actually spend your time, (2) how you should spend it, and (3) how you can improve the ways you spend it.

Setting Your Own Hours

One of the joys of free-lancing is the freedom to set your own hours. A few free-lancers keep unusual hours, but most settle into a fairly regular work schedule. "Fairly regular hours" usually translate into something resembling the nine-to-five workday, if for no other reason than because that is when the rest of the world works. If clients need to call you, they will do so then. If you need to call them or want to solicit new business, that is when you must do it. Margaret Stein said she had a tendency to maintain those hours from the very beginning, except when she was besieged with work. She recalled, "The very first day I worked at home, I was very diligent. I had planned to work long, hard hours. I didn't have on a watch—a sign of my new freedom that I soon dispensed with—but I felt myself growing very tired. I guessed it was about 7:00 or 7:30 at night. I threw down my pencil and decided to give up for the day. To my surprise, it was 5:00 P.M. on the nose." Barbara Zimmerman said: "I try to work nine to five, but I also have a trade-off. I use the freedom I have to do errands, so I make up for it by working a little late or on weekends." Many free-lancers, such as Bryan Johnson, rise early to take advantage of the hours of the morning before the phone starts ringing. He noted, "I often start work at 5:00 or 6:00 in the morning, so I can work for about six hours and then go do something else in the afternoon." Like busy executives, a free-lancer soon discovers that even an hour in the morning before the phone rings can be precious.

If you are going to be a successful free-lancer, you should undertake the management of your time as seriously as you possibly can. Time-management consultants often refer to the 80-20 rule, which reflects their discovery that in business, people tend to spend about 80 percent of their time on tasks that produce about 20 percent of the work. Too many people work diligently on low-value activities. These activities may make them feel very good when completed, but they aren't real work. Often, office workers, who are basically at the beck and call of their superiors or at the mercy of the corporation's demands for paperwork, have no choice. As a free-lancer, though, you do have a choice. You will find that with planning and discipline you can learn to fill the hours of your day with meaningful work—the kind that brings in a paycheck on a regular basis. One free-lancer, when asked how she maintained the self-discipline to work in her home day after day, year after year, commented, "I find that what I do during the day is so directly related to how much food I have on the table that I have no problem in getting the work done."

Time-wasters

The Small Business Administration has published a list of time-wasters. Generally, they break them down into external or internal categories. Of the external time wasters, the following apply to free-lancers:

Telephone calls
Meetings
Visitors
Socializing
Lack of information
Communication breakdown
Excessive paperwork

Of the internal time-wasters, these particularly apply to free-lancers:

Procrastination
Failure to delegate tasks and responsibilities
Unclear goals
Failure to set priorities
Crisis management
Failure to plan work
Poor scheduling
Trying to do too much in too short a time
Lack of self-discipline
Lack of relevant skills

With some careful thought on how you do handle your time and an ongoing review of your work methods, you can avoid all these pitfalls. Here are some general hints on managing your time:

- Figure out what time of day you are most productive and make sure you schedule important work during those hours. Margaret Stein said: "I'm really a morning person, but that is always when the phone rings. I bought myself a phone machine, turned my phone down so I couldn't hear it ring, and I never answer the phone until 11:00 A.M., at which time I have done about four hours of work."

- Keep a detailed log of how you spend your time. Record your activities for every quarter hour. You will quickly see when and how you waste time, and you will probably be able to spot your most productive hours if you are not aware of them.

- If the log shows a lack of self-discipline, create new time-management habits. Write a fairly rigid schedule for yourself, and stick to it until it becomes habit.

- Keep a calendar, preferably covering a week at a time, so you can always see what you have to do. Many free-lancers keep a large desk calendar for scheduling and long-term planning, and then carry a smaller one with them in which to write appointments and make short lists.

There are also some specific things you can do to manage your time more wisely:

- Do similar tasks at one time; for example, do all your telephoning at once or all your letters at one time.

- Relegate the small or routine tasks to your least productive hours. That is when you should write letters (unless it is a very important letter) or make phone calls.

- Get someone else to do work you don't absolutely have to do. Lots of free-lancers refuse to consider that they might need office help or an assistant of some kind. If you are spending much of your time on routine tasks and too little on your real work, then it is time to think about hiring someone. Get a student to type letters two hours a week, hire someone to do your routine research for you on an hourly basis, even think about hiring someone to clean your home (and office) so you don't have to be distracted by that kind of work.

• Use downtime—when you are riding on a bus or waiting for an appointment—to do certain routine or easy tasks, such as figuring your expense account, reviewing a memo for a meeting, looking at the morning mail, or reading trade journals and magazines.

• Speaking of the morning mail, resist the urge to do something to it right away. It will always contain something that will make you want to type an immediate response or pick up the phone, but if you have planned to do such routine work later in the day, then stick to your schedule. Learn to toss out junk mail without reading it.

• Control paper. Keep your systems simple; always look for ways to streamline.

• Keep things where they belong. That way you will always be able to find them when you need them. And keep them in logical places. If you use a certain file five times a day, it makes no sense to put it in a file drawer after each use. Keep it nearby or on your desk.

• Get a good contacts file, one that rests right by your phone. Cross-reference numbers that you use a lot. For example, if you fly to Boston every few weeks, cross-reference all the Boston airlines on one general card and then put specific information such as phone numbers and flight information on separate entry cards.

• Whenever you use a telephone number for the first time, consider whether or not you should add it to your permanent phone file.

• Put any information that you need while you are on the phone on the main card. If you work with someone whose assistant always answers the phone, note the assistant's name. A phone card should contain not only the phone number but also the complete name, title, and address of the person.

• Use a timer, if need be, to break up your day into specific tasks, especially if you are trying to train yourself to new work habits.

Making Long-range Plans

Setting goals and planning your work in advance can help you accomplish work in the long run. Long-range planning should be done on a yearly basis, although you should also keep track of monthly earnings for the sake of your cash flow. One free-lance writer tried to set up her schedule on an annual basis: "Every fall I try to set myself up for the rest of the year. I write several short book proposals, knowing that two or three will sell. Beyond that, I usually have a long-term book I'm working on over a period of several years. Then I scout around for one or two major rewriting projects from textbook publishers. That pretty much fills my year. People tell me I'm lucky to be able to set up my year that way, but I work very hard for several months to get all that done. And of course, some years things do not fall into place. That can work both ways. One year, I sold too many little books—I was busy every minute."

One free-lance design consultant said her financial life was a shambles until she learned to think in terms of yearly planning. She reported, "I have a small regular job as a design consultant; it takes about three days a month and pays $500, or $6,000 a year. Then I also am the designer of a small magazine published by a museum; that brings in $2,000 a year. Beyond that base of $8,000, I have learned that I can count on $5,000 to $6,000 in freelance art catalogues a year— they are my real love. I actively look for another $8,000 to $10,000 in miscellaneous design projects—any kind will do— to round out my year."

A free-lance financial consultant discussed even more long-range financial planning. He said, "I keep the books for two companies, each of which pays me $15,000 a year. I do this work in their offices, though, and it takes about half my time. Eventually, I want my entire business to be run out of my home and to consist of private clients. Presently, I am picking up another $15,000 in private clients each year. For the last three years, this has escalated by 100 percent. When I started three years ago, I only did $5,000 in private business. My problem is planning when to let one of the companies go since each represents a sizable chunk of income to me. I've decided to hire someone to help me with the private clients so I can increase my volume by more than 100 percent. This way, I figure I can drop one of the companies two years from now and the second company a couple of years later."

Keeping Lists

On a simple level, one way to initiate long-range time planning is to make A, B, and C lists. There are several ways to do this, and you must find the one that suits you. You might draw up an A list of things that are most pressing to get done in one day, a B list for things that are important but can be done over a week or so, and a C list for long-term planning projects. You can also draw up an A list for things that must be done immediately, a B list for things that are not pressing, and a C list for things that really don't need handling. Either way, these lists will give you a sense of perspective.

When thinking about long-range plans, try to put your ideas in writing. It will help you consider them more seriously. A project that sounds wonderful in your head may not be so great or even possible once you commit it to paper. Here is a way to draw up a plan you are considering:

1. Define the problem or describe the project.

2. Describe possible course of action.

3. Describe the pros and cons of that course of action.

4. Consider the alternatives.

5. Review all possible courses of action.

6. Decide on best course of action.

This list can be used for things as diverse as deciding whether or not to hire someone to work for you, figuring out whether a work project is feasible, or deciding whether or not to invest in new office equipment. It can even be used if you are planning a new way to structure your day.

Once you have given yourself a red or green light on a project or plan, you need to schedule it—at least as much as you can. Free-lancers often find that the nature of their work—which largely consists in waiting for others to give them work—is such that they often cannot schedule projects as well as they might like to. One free-lancer commented, "That's the hard thing about free-lance publishing. Nothing runs on schedule. Books are supposed to come, and they don't. I used to set up for projects before they came in, but they rarely came in on schedule. The only way I will block out time now is if I have a written agreement with someone to the effect that I will still be paid even if the work does not come in on time. If I can substitute another project, I do, and then I don't charge the client. If I can't, the client owes me. It gets to be a juggling act, though."

Before you can schedule specific projects, you need to know how much time you will have to spend on administrative tasks such as maintaining contact with old clients and soliciting new ones, correspondence, and routine office chores. How much time will you have to give over to paperwork? If you have kept a log for a week or two, you should have no trouble pinpointing how much time is needed for this or any other activity.

Writing a Production Schedule

Offices go round on production schedules, at least well-run ones do. Free-lancers often think they can do without them. Nothing could be further from the truth. Especially if you are juggling more than one project, you need a production schedule that lists the materials you will need, steps that will be required to complete the project, and an estimate of the amount of time you will need to complete each step of the project. The hardest part of any project is calculating the amount of time that you must spend at each step along the way.

There are several ways to determine how much time you will need, and often a combination of these techniques works. You can ask the client how much time he thinks will be required. You might think that you must take his response with a grain of salt since it will be to his advantage to underestimate the number of hours you will need to work, but in many kinds of free-lancing, free-lancers reported that their clients had a realistic and often generous grasp of the number of hours involved in the projects they assigned. The key is whether or not the client has done the kind of work he is asking you to do. If he has, then he probably knows how long it will take. If he hasn't, then he not only doesn't know but you may not even want to give him a chance to mull it over. Two other ways are better for figuring out the time that will be required for a project: Ask your colleagues how much time they think will be necessary, or do a little work on the assignment and project the time you will need based on that.

Even with the very best production schedules, plans often go awry. As a free-lancer you will never have the control you may need or would like to have, over your work flow. You can spend a lot of time fighting this, or you can try to maintain some flexibility.

An Added Benefit of Advance Planning

There is one other benefit to making short- and long-term plans. In a purely psychological sense and in a very real economic sense, they can help to alleviate some of the insecurity associated with free-lancing. If you have scheduled your future projects in writing, you will have a clear idea of when it is time to go after more work and how much work you will need to stay solvent.

GETTING ORGANIZED

All free-lancers need to be organized. There are, of course, people who work on desks stacked high with paper and projects, but the only people who work successfully in such cluttered surroundings are those who can immediately put their hands on anything they need. If you have to search for something, you are too disorganized. And disorganization has never helped any free-lancer become successful. So even if you are the type who is happy surrounded by clutter, make sure it is organized clutter.

Your office should be organized so the things you use regularly are readily accessible. Keep files and reference books near where you work. Also take time to clear out your files regularly. As a free-lancer you will find there will be little that you have to hang onto over the years. Unless you took a course in filing, expect to play around with a filing system until you settle on something that works for you. And be prepared to rethink your files occasionally. Too many people make the mistake of setting up an office and viewing it as permanent. Instead, think of your office as a living thing, at least in terms of how you organize it. Rethink your organizational systems occasionally even if it means taking them apart and starting all over.

Learn to control paper flow. Start by doing something with paper right away. For example, if you clip from newspapers and magazines, set up a file to hold the clippings until you find time to sort them out and file them. When you read your mail, sort it into several stacks: things you must handle right away, things you can handle within a week, and things you need never handle. The last stack goes directly to the wastecan.

Keep a note pad near you as you work to jot down things as you think of them. Resist the urge to jump up and do them; just note that they must be done and when.

If your work requires it, get a bulletin board and hang it near your desk. It is an excellent place to display a calendar on which you mark deadlines, as well as production schedules and work-flow charts.

Get in and out baskets if that will help you control the flow of work across your desk. Even in and out baskets, though, tend to become swollen with papers that are never sorted, so you might want to take a hint from free-lance editors, who often arrange their projects on a shelf or work table. Don't be afraid to be slightly or even greatly unorthodox as you think about how to organize your desk and office. This isn't a corporation, or if it is, it's your own corporation.

KEEPING THE WORLD AT BAY

Desk organized? Work planned for the next five years? Calendar diligently marked with little and big projects over the next two months? Then the next step is to keep the world at bay so you can get some serious work done. Learning to take the time that you need to work is one of the hardest things for a free-lancer to do. As Judy Waggoner noted, "There are always the unexpected things that come up: a sick child, a long telephone conversation, other responsibilities such as shopping or chauffeuring."

Free-lancers are sitting ducks for friends who have a little extra time on their hands. They know your boss won't pop in the door and give you the evil eye for yakking when you should be working. And in all honesty, since most free-lancing is essentially lonely work, free-lancers don't exactly flinch when the phone rings—even at the busiest time of day. Despite all this, the day will come when you simply must work without interruption. Or when, if you love your work, you will want to work without interruption. What can you do about it? There are several things.

Controlling the Phone

First, you must control the telephone. A friend when you are lonely, it is a monster when you are busy. Start by making all your outgoing calls at one time of day. If possible, tell people to call you at a certain time of day. Note: This applies more to friends than clients, but you can even suggest to clients that you are most easily reached at specific hours. Turn on the phone machine and turn off the phone. That way you won't hear the phone ring, and you will get all your messages. If you have an answering service, tell them to pick up on the first ring.

Avoiding the Office Time-wasters

People in offices spend an enormous amount of time in meetings and writing reports and memos. Mostly useless time. If you are not careful, you too will spend an enormous amount of time doing the same thing. People will always be trying to hook you into their office routine. Either they think you miss it, and they want to include you, or they want you to be as frazzled and unproductive as they are. Either way, don't let it happen to you. To avoid meetings:

• Send your agent.

• Go but announce that you can only stay for a short while. Announce when you have to leave when you arrive or when you schedule the meeting. Not only will this keep the meeting short, but this kind of time limitation will cut down immensely on the small talk that consumes much of meetings.

• Don't go to a meeting to discuss something you can handle over the phone. And don't handle something over the phone that you can handle in a letter, or the reverse, if it is true. If you can work faster over the phone than in writing, then always pick up the phone before resorting to a letter.

Saying No

There are three times when you should say no to a client. The first is when you are too busy. You should also say no when you don't know how to do something. It is no use trying to sell talents and skills you don't have. The only result will be that you will get jobs from people who will never hire you again. That is a loss you can never recoup in free-lancing. Finally, you should say no when someone is taking advantage of you. By nature many free-lancers are quiet, passive people—that is the kind of person who does especially well working alone. Yet if you are going to survive in free-lancing, you will have to throw off enough of your passivity to say no to someone who is not using you well. One free-lance editor finally got the nerve to say no to a client who underpaid her when she had developed enough skill to get higher rates from other publishers. A free-lance costume designer says she won't work with a producer who doesn't give her enough money to do a project well: "I'm much more likely to quibble over the budget I need to do a job well than my salary. I've let projects fall through over that issue."

When you do say no, do it graciously. If you say no because you lack the skills, let the client feel you would like to be kept in mind for future projects. Also try to mention what you do handle well so the client will know what to call you for.

FREE-LANCERS' PITFALLS

There are some pitfalls in free-lancing that are not normally encountered in other kinds of work. Free-lancers universally acknowledge what they are: procrastination and loneliness. Procrastination, often the result of loneliness, is especially disastrous. Anyone can procrastinate, but only a free-lancer can go to two movies in a row on a bad day. And people who procrastinate on the boss's time usually try to cover their tracks to some extent with legitimate work. Free-lancers just lose the time.

When You Cannot Work

When you hit a day, or even a few days, when you simply cannot bring yourself to work or when nothing good happens when you try to be productive, the best way to deal with this is directly. Go easy on yourself; it happens to everyone. Acknowledge that you are—at the moment—burned out.

Plan a change of pace. Take an early or a late lunch. Go to two movies, only don't let yourself feel guilty about it. Or do, if it will help when you start work again. Take a walk. Call someone for a chat—preferably someone who works in an office, not a fellow free-lancer, who will be unable to resist you and thus may also lose valuable work time. If quitting time is near, knock off early.

Fighting yourself on the days when you can't work only causes you to lose more time in the long run. Stein commented, "I never used to give myself permission to go do something else when I couldn't get my work done, but then I realized that I wasted the time one way or another anyway. Now, when I see that I really can't work, I take off for an hour or so."

Lee concurred: "A friend who also free-lances asks where it is written that we should work nine to five. Another friend even reminded me that people in offices don't work thirty-five hours every week. And I forget to take into consideration the nights when I work until eight and on weekends."

The Loneliness of the Longtime Free-lancer

It would be nice to report that only new free-lancers get lonely, bored, or suffer from feelings of isolation. Unfortunately, it is an occupational hazard suffered by practically all free-lancers off and on. Even free-lancers who deal with people all day suffer from the isolation and occasional boredom. Artist's agent Julie Jensen found this was true: "I have a lot of contact with people since I call on gallery managers all day and spend several nights each week seeing people professionally. But those aren't friends, with a few exceptions. It's not even a particularly friendly world. There are nights when I just know I have to see or talk to a friend if I'm going to feel at all human." A writer who worked long hours alone commented, "I've trained all my friends never to break dinner dates with me. They know I may not have seen another human face for forty-eight hours. I love my work, I like working alone, but yes, I get lonely and need to be with other people simply because I haven't been for a while."

Lest you give up free-lancing before you even start, there are things you can do to fight the free-lancers' pitfalls:

- Make sure you get out every day. One free-lance commodities broker who had to start every day with a careful reading of several newspapers was frequently asked why he didn't just subscribe, rather than head out in all kinds of weather to buy the papers. He said, "Not often, but sometimes, that outing to buy the paper is the only time I get out all day. I wouldn't dream of having my morning papers waiting for me on the stoop."

- Intersperse errands with your work. Remember that one of the joys of free-lancing is that you never have to go to the grocery store at 5:00 P.M. when the lines are long.

- Make friends or find colleagues in the neighborhood so you will have someone to call for a quick lunch on the spur of the moment.

- If you live in a city where others do the same kind of work you do, organize a group to meet regularly for lunch. For several years, writers on the Upper West Side of New York (where writers are about as common as the brownstones that line the narrow side streets) met weekly at a local pub to discuss or not discuss their business, but certainly for the company.

- Extend yourself to get to know the local business owners. You may not want to have lunch with your dry cleaner, but a quick conversation with him can take the edge off a lonely day.

- Put a reward system into effect on lonely or nonproductive days. Work several hours, then knock off to go to the movies or for a walk. Or have a nice lunch and get some exercise, and more often than not, you will find yourself mentally prepared to get back to work.

- Let yourself fantasize about the possibilities of success. How would it feel if you got a project earning twice as much as you've ever earned before? If you became a star on Broadway? If *The New York Times* said you were the foremost costume designer of the decade? If your book started climbing the best-sellers list? If you landed a big gallery show? Don't get too carried away with fantasy, though, or you will fantasize yourself right out of a career.

- Change your work routine. Try working in the afternoon and handling your managerial problems in the morning for a few days, or vice versa. Or sleep late and work later in the day.

- Even though the opposite tactic was suggested earlier, try interspersing several small projects among the large ones just for a change of pace.

- Finally, don't forget to leave some time for planning your personal life, for meditation, and for thoughts of your future. Too many successful free-lancers keep themselves on rigid schedules and account for every single minute of their workdays. Unfortunately, this can be the fastest road to burnout.

Burnout

It happens to teachers, business executives, advertising executives. People who work in high-pressure jobs. It also happens to free-lancers, but it scares them more because they often must continue working to meet the monthly bills. So what do you do when loneliness and procrastination turns into burnout? A free-lance writer who experienced his first—and he hoped, his last—bout with burnout, shared his thoughts on the subject, "I had just finished a book I'd been working on for four years. I was inert. I had lots of work to do and was afraid I couldn't get any of it done. I didn't have the money to flee the country for a six-week vacation. I knew I had to self-prescribe in this situation. I started by talking about it to my friends, who were amazingly sympathetic. They had all seen it coming on, and they encouraged me to accept it and scale down the amount of work I did over the next few months. Fortunately, I was able to do that. I earned a little less, but I'll have a longer work life as a result."

Another free-lancer described her tactic for fighting burnout, "I don't know if this would work for everyone or not, but I use strenuous exercise to combat burnout. The combination of more time to myself and a way to burn off my anxiety seems to do the trick for me."

Each person has to develop his or her own solution to burnout—and the solution for free-lancers often is based on financial need. If you cannot cut back on work, then consider a part-time job doing something totally different for a few months. That way, you can still carry on some of your free-lance work and think over whether or not it is time for you to do something else. While you are thinking, you will also be rejuvenating. And the day will come when you will be ready to do your serious work again. One good thing about burnout that is rarely pointed out in the books and articles on the subject: It need not be permanent unless you decide to make it so.

The Art of Expansion

10

Successful free-lancers often report that the well runs dry when they least expect it. One free-lancer spoke of his dismay when this happened to him, "I had set everything up right, made lots of cold calls, and followed up every possible lead. I enjoyed a healthy free-lance business for two years. In fact, I never made new calls after the first round that I made to set up my business. People came to me, and it was very nice, since I don't like selling myself, but then, who does? Then one fall, right after a very busy summer, I had no work lined up. I was finishing a project, and for the first time in two years, I wasn't booked months, or even weeks, in advance."

While this free-lancer's business may appear to have dried up for no reason, there is something he neglected to do: Solicit new business. It's a basic rule of free-lancing that no matter how busy you are, you should never fail to set aside some time to make sales calls either to potential new clients or to renew ties with regular clients.

The second basic rule of free-lancing is that you should always be prepared for the possibility that you may have to find and expand into new markets. One free-lancer, who had also enjoyed several prosperous years before her business began to slip, reported, "I did continually solicit new business from my regular clients. When I met someone new, I always checked to see if they needed my services. I checked out old clients I hadn't heard from twice a year. But then, despite all my efforts, I hit a slow period. I began to realize that I had rounded up as much business from my present clients as I was going to get. No one else did what I did, so I didn't even have to worry about competition. But the market just wasn't large enough to support me full-time the way I had come to expect to support myself. That's when I started looking around for ways to expand my business into new but, I hoped, related markets."

Although enough emphasis cannot be placed on the need to be constantly on the lookout for new business and potential markets, there are also some warning signals that should alert you to the need to do some planning for the future of your business. You need to begin an active campaign to find new business when sales have fallen off slowly over the long term, and you do not think this trend will reverse itself. This is a rather extreme example, but it makes the point: Over the last twenty or thirty years, the major magazine sources have dried up for short stories. Persons who were able to support themselves writing short stories in the 1940s and even into the 1950s can no longer do that in the 1980s. There are few signs that the market will reverse itself, despite occasional plans to rejuvenate literary magazines that cater to this market. Because of television, among other factors, the market for short stories will probably never be as strong as it once was. Writers who want to write short stories, therefore, must also look for additional means of supporting themselves. They need new markets. Many fields have been taken over or drastically changed by technology. If yours is one of those rapidly changing fields, then you must also be prepared to look for new clients.

Recessionary times are another time to think about looking

for new business. In many businesses free-lancers do well during a recession because companies tend to cut back on their staffs and use free-lance services. (Of course, this also means that there are more persons working as free-lancers and that you must compete with ex-staffers.) When you see a recession ahead, make plans to compete in that kind of market. Usually this means expanding the number or type of clients for whom you work so you will not suffer any serious financial harm if one of your regular clients decides to cut back on your services.

You need to find new business when you are not earning enough money—and you do not see the prospects for earning enough money—to live on if your work flow continues at the same level. Sometimes you don't know you can't earn enough at a particular free-lance career until you have worked at it for a couple of years. It is easy to attribute low earnings in the start-up years to the fact that you are just beginning. Eventually, though, you have to earn enough to be satisfied, and if this does not appear to be a possibility, then you must look around—certainly for new clients and probably for new markets.

Inflation also takes its toll on everyone's paycheck. If you are not earning enough, not through any shortcomings of your own but simply because everything costs more, you still have to do something about it. What you will have to do is solicit new business and possibly look for new markets. The hard thing is not figuring out when to look for new business; it is figuring out how to go about it.

The first step is to draw up a plan of action. The research, planning, and goal setting required to expand your business or push into new markets are not all that different from what you did when you initially set up your free-lance business.

THINKING ABOUT EXPANSION

Begin by honestly evaluating your present position as well as what the future is liable to bring. There is no point to expanding into areas that you do not particularly enjoy or where you have little aptitude. Besides, doing work you want to do is what the independence of free-lancing is all about.

Free-lancer Judy Waggoner, who had begun as a typist and expanded into copy-editing when she realized she had strengths in that area that she was not tapping, found after several years of working in publishing that she needed to look around yet again for new markets. Waggoner lived in a town where there was a limited amount of publishing. Because she had a husband and children, she could not consider relocating to a major publishing center. Thus, when one of her major clients was sold and moved to another city, she found herself with an unanticipated gap in her earnings. She considered which parts of her free-lance business she did best, and soon realized that she was extremely good at detailed work and that she had an unusually logical and orderly mind. After reading as much as she could about the various kinds of jobs in publishing and talking with colleagues, Waggoner decided that she would like to give indexing a try. It drew on her strengths; and she had no competition in her city (publishers had been sending work to New York indexers). Waggoner discussed the possibility of moving into indexing with several colleagues, all of whom offered as much advice as they could. From these conversations, she decided that she could teach herself to index. Her next step was one that should be familiar to all free-lancers: a bluff. Before she even had a chance to bill herself as an indexer (and after several months of practice), someone called her to ask if, by any chance, she knew how to index. She said yes, conferred with a colleague in New York to learn the going rate, and found that she had her first job as an indexer. Thanks to her alertness to the need to expand and her willingness to train for new areas, Waggoner now functioned as a free-lance typist, copy editor, and indexer.

Free-lancer Joe Reilly was struggling to earn a living as a set designer. When things went sour, due to a run of cancelled projects that Reilly had no control over, he decided he needed another source of income, if only for a few months. Reilly considered what he was happiest doing and realized that he most enjoyed drafting plans for stage sets. Armed with this knowledge about himself, he went out and found free-lance work as an architect's draftsman.

There are other things in addition to your personal strengths that must be considered as you plan a move to attract new business or find new markets:

- Do you want to stay in the industry you are in? Barbara Lee, photographer's representative, has no immediate plans to move, but she knows that she does not want to live in New York City for many more years. And although she enjoys the high earnings of her present business and knows that she will always free-lance, she has begun to investigate careers that could be pursued outside New York City. So far she has not found her niche, but she has established some standards. First, she doesn't like recordkeeping, so the business she enters next must be something she can run on a cash basis with little need for recordkeeping. She loves animals, so she is looking for some service related to animal care that she could provide. Janet Rish, on the other hand, loves the free-lance consulting she does in museums, where she helps to set up shows. The pay is low, though, and so she needs to expand in the same business. She is considering how to approach corporations with art collections who could use her services.

- Are you willing to travel to find new markets? Often free-lancers tend to forget that there are potential markets everywhere. One enterprising public-relations expert who worked in the beauty business in New York also saw the possibility of free-lancing for small salons in nearby cities such as Philadelphia or Baltimore. The response to her direct mail flyer came from Washington, D.C., and now she thinks of her monthly jaunts to Washington as one of the perks of her job. Conversely, an excellent free-lance editor who specialized in sailing books and lived in Washington, D.C., found her specialized market could be tapped in New York. She made twice-monthly trips to New York to keep in touch with her clients there.

- How much money will you need to capture a new market? Usually, costs for expansion efforts can be kept low. If you need a great deal of money, or more than you have or can raise, then you may have to abandon a possible market and look for something else.

- Do you have enough time? If you are expanding because you cannot earn a good living in your present field, then you may hurt yourself even more if you cut back on the number of hours you work so you can devote yourself to your expansion efforts. The trick is to expand into areas that will not require huge amounts of time, or to grit your teeth and accept the fact that you will live a little poorer than you want to for yet another start-up period.

- Will you need new equipment? Expansion may not be feasible if you need to invest in major pieces of equipment. If possible, consider renting equipment you need to go into a new area until you see the first signs of success. And before you consider moving into an area that requires major changes in equipment, think about whether you are using your present equipment to its fullest capacity.

- Your final consideration should be how much you can earn. Never move into a new market simply because you will be good at it or because it interests you without first exploring how much money you can make in it. Most expansions are prompted by financial need, and you should never overlook the fact that this is your primary concern.

BUILDING A CUSTOMER PROFILE

Another thing you should do before you expand is to build a customer profile. When you started free-lancing you drew up a prospective customer profile; now you need to draw one describing who your customers turned out to be. To do this, begin by (1) listing all your clients and (2) dividing the list into active and inactive clients, if possible. Then analyze the following:

1. Have you developed any special expertise, based on the customers who seek you out? In other words, why do you have the customers you have?

2. Why have you lost customers? Be honest. Was your work unsatisfactory? Did the customer's needs change so much that your services were no longer required? Did the competition offer some service you could not provide? Did you have to charge too much?

3. What trends can you spot in your present customer's businesses? How will these trends affect the need for your services?

4. Do you want to regain the customers you lost? Never overlook this as a possibility. Free-lancers always have some customers who are inactive simply because they have not been called on for a while. On the other hand, perhaps you prefer to find new customers?

5. Which customers pay you the most? Can you expand that type of customer?

6. Which customers pay you the least? Can you afford to drop them so you can make room for higher-paying customers?

DEVELOPING AN EXPANSION PLAN

By now, you will have some idea of what direction you might move. Here is how to put it in writing and consider the pros and cons of such a move:

1. Describe in writing why you feel you need to expand.

2. Describe your present services.

3. Describe your market or sales history, mainly in terms of the ups and downs.

4. Describe the financial outlook for your profession as you see it. What lies ahead? What is different from a year ago?

5. Draw up several courses of action, that is, areas you might expand into, new customers you might solicit.

6. Consider the pros and cons of each possibility.

7. Make a decision for a course of action based on the information you have accumulated.

Remember that if one plan of action does not work out, you can always return to this expansion plan and reconsider alternate courses of action. What you choose to do today may be based on such things as how much time you can spend finding new business or your inability to invest in new equipment at the present time, but a year from now those elements could be completely different.

Possibilities for Expansion

Although any individual free-lancer must make a personal decision regarding the area of expansion or new market that is right for him or her, there are some general areas for making more money that are open to all free-lancers. Many free-lancers can look into the following as sources of extra money:

Teaching
Grants
Prizes
Lectures or performances
Corporate sales
Consulting

Information about teaching jobs, grants, and prizes is often available through reading professional journals or at conventions. The foundations directory, available in most libraries, may also provide information about monies available in your field. While you are at the library, ask the librarian if she or he can recommend any other sources of information to you. Professional organizations can also sometimes supply information on part-time or full-time teaching jobs, grants, and prizes.

If you decide you want to give lectures or performances, you must build up contacts among persons with the power to help you obtain speaking or performing engagements. Some media agencies that handle writers and show-business personalities also specialize in arranging lecture tours, and private publicists will also take on individual clients for a fee. Among your informal contacts, as a rule, it is better to wait until you are asked to lecture or perform, but there is nothing wrong with letting others know that you are interested.

The last two items on the above list may prove to be especially important to free-lancers in the 1980s, when there will probably be less government money around for grants and as teaching jobs diminish. These are corporate sales and consulting. Both enable you to turn a substantial profit; the only drawback is the highly commercial nature of the work—which may be just what you want. Business writing, for example, an area open to most editors and writers, pays as high as $100 to $800 a day; hourly rates can run as high as $50 to $100 compared to $10 to $20 for comparable work for publishers. Photographers can often sell their services to businesses that produce annual reports or other publications. Designers and typesetters can also sell their services directly to corporations. People with any kind of specialty in business can often become consultants; for that matter, persons with any kind of specialty at all can consult in their chosen fields. Architects, nurses and physicians, scientists, and academics are among those to whom the field of consulting is wide open.

Many free-lancers do not seek out corporate business because they do not know how to do so, but the methods used to establish yourself in publishing or any other business are the same ones you should use to move into consulting and corporate work. In addition, here are some pointers for moving into the corporate world:

- Build on your present skills. For example, do you edit or write in such areas as psychology or time management? Then call corporations in these fields and sell yourself as someone who already has the expertise in their areas.

- To find corporate or consulting business, watch trends in a specific business that interests you just as you do for your present business. Buy professional magazines and journals; read the business pages of your local newspaper and *The Wall Street Journal*. Trend spotting, a sort of sixth sense that all successful free-lancers eventually develop, can easily be applied in any area.

- Before you call on a corporation, check it out so you can talk intelligently about it. Begin by reading its annual report and any other literature it issues about itself. Many corporations can also be checked by looking up their listing in Standard and Poors, Dun and Bradstreet, or more specialized listings. Ask the librarian at your local library to help you.

- Never be afraid to go big. Always go to top management with your ideas, or at least go to someone who has the power to buy your services. Don't worry about going too high. You can always be referred downward through the ranks; what is not so easy is getting away from someone who feels flattered by your attention but has no power to use your services.

There are also some things to keep in mind whether you are expanding into corporate circles or courting new clients in your original field.

- Look for new groups to join, so you can expand your circle of contacts. Are you an author? Join a group of magazine writers. A painter? Join a group of artists planning a major exhibit of drawings. A furniture designer? Join a lecture series planned for architects. The possibilities are limitless once you start to look into them.

- Consider taking jobs that do not pay much but which will serve to spread your name around to new potential clients or new markets. Get yourself listed on the masthead of a trade publication as a consulting editor or contributor. The trick, of course, is to find jobs that also do not require much work of you.

- If you have moved away from your original markets, consider returning to them. You will bring fresh insights and ideas that may make you more valuable than you were the first time around. Sometimes, too, companies that hire free-lancers simply need a break. They may falsely think your competition is better simply because they are new faces. So you take a breather, too, and then come back—as a new face.

- Be conservative—most of the time—when planning expansion. This is the opposite of advice that is usually given to business-school graduates, who are taught that they should spend whatever is necessary to do the job right. That philosophy is fine when you are spending the boss's money; when you are the boss, however, a little conservatism not only pays off but it may be your only option. If possible, set aside some extra money to support your expansion efforts, along with some money to live on while you get back on your feet should you find that you have moved in the wrong direction.

- Expansion and soliciting new business is not all action. Take some time—a couple of weeks, if need be—to sit back and ponder your fate. You can often save a lot of money, time, and effort simply by thinking before you act.

Dealing with Present Clients During Expansion

While you are in the process of moving yourself on to greater glory, do not neglect the people who have been hiring you all along. Rarely will you want to give them up entirely, so your only alternative is to continue to service their accounts while you develop new ones. There is an art to servicing regular clients, though. Do not overservice bread-and-butter accounts, meaning those regular ones who will use you no matter what you do. They are not in the wine-and-dine category because they are already there for you. Do continue, however, to give regular clients very good service.

Do not overservice marginal accounts, either. One free-lancer who specialized in writing textbooks by teaming up with someone who had expert knowledge but needed a writer came to the realization that she was courting some of her clients far too much. The jobs she went after were big, often involving sizable advances and a 50 percent cut on royalties, so they did require some courting, which might be drawn out over several months before a deal was struck. Often, though, prospective clients, which included publishers and academics, came to her before they really had a go-ahead on a project. She soon learned to be polite but to give these people a minimal amount of her time until they had something concrete to discuss.

On the other hand, the cultivation of customers is for a free-lancer an ongoing activity. In a service business you can get business simply by acquiring a reputation for doing excellent work, but first, people must know that you are good. You must constantly maintain a profile that is at least as high as that of your competition.

MARKETING YOURSELF

Expansion opens the doors to three activities you may not have considered before: marketing, advertising, and publicity. Marketing is the overall plan that you develop for selling yourself; it involves spotting your market—your potential customers—and working out a plan for selling them your services. Advertising, which, like publicity, should be part of a marketing plan, is something you usually pay for; it is direct mail brochures, ads in journals and trade newspapers, and anything else you do along those lines to tout your services.

Publicity is advertising you get for free—short write-ups or articles in newspapers or magazines, interviews on talk shows, free plugs on radio or television.

Creating Your Image

Marketing is a tricky business for almost all kinds of free-lancers. Most are too small to advertise or publicize in any major way. One aspect of marketing involves the development of the image that you present to your clients. Corporations spend huge sums of money on their images; fortunately, there is no need for you to do this as a free-lancer. You need only to give some thought to how you want to present yourself. The possibilities for labeling free-lancers are many; here are only three:

Messy but creative
Businesslike and organized
Casual and informal

All of these images could work, depending upon the kind of service you offer. A commercial artist or graphic designer, for example, might easily get away with a certain amount of disorganization and messiness (about his business, not about the kind of work he turns in). Persons who hire this kind of free-lancer often think more of them because they display these seemingly "creative" characteristics. Interestingly, you can overdo the dress-for-success image, too. Several in-house editors said they were put off with free-lancers whose image was very formal and businesslike, particularly in terms of dress. One noted, "I prefer to think that a free-lancer has just popped in to pick up my assignment and is heading right home to begin work on it. Someone who is too dressed up looks too social to me, and likewise, someone who is too casually dressed. I'm always nervous when an editor shows up dressed as if he or she is headed for the beach or a baseball game."

Beyond creating an image for yourself or letting an image emerge, consider what you want to do in the way of advertising and publicity. As a general rule, unless you are going after big corporate money, keep everything small and unostentatious. Free-lancers trade on being small independent operators, and that is mostly how their clients like to think of them. If you start to look too big or too fancy, as may well happen if you turn to fancy letterheads and cards or four-color brochures about yourself, clients may shy away. They will tell themselves that you are too expensive (without even checking to find out) or that they can just as easily hire a large corporation or company as they can someone who is trying to look like one.

The first step in developing a marketing plan is to ask around and find out what other free-lancers in your business do. Don't wear blinders, though. Just because some free-lancers do nothing to announce their presence does not mean that you should follow suit. If you talk to enough colleagues, you will get some sort of consensus about the limits of marketing yourself.

If marketing is acceptable in the area where you free-lance, then you should consider it. Generally you should bill yourself as a specialist even if you happen to be a generalist. There is such a thing as scaring away clients by giving them the idea that you will take on anything and everything. One free-lancer who functions as a haircutter, dress designer, and sound consultant keeps his careers very separate for this reason. Another free-lance copy editor who also does indexing prepares separate flyers to send to her clients. She advertises only one specialty at a time.

Marketing—How Much Is Enough?

When planning a marketing campaign, be realistic about what you can spend—and recognize that you need not spend very much. You are not trying to mold a corporate image; you are trying to get clients to buy your services. If you find yourself planning to buy a color, half-page ad in a trade magazine when everyone else who does the kind of work you do only buys small 1½-inch-square ads, then consider your motives. Are you doing this because it will result in business, or because it will make you feel important? The same thing applies to free-lancers who seek newspaper publicity. Will it really get you business, or does it simply feel exciting to go after this kind of notice from others? Undeniably, some free-lance businesses are built around a well-placed newspaper story or ad campaign, but is yours one of them? One publicist, well known in her field of plastics, struck out on her own suddenly when she and her employers reached an impasse and she resigned rather unexpectedly. Since she knew how to do publicity, she started planning a campaign, but before she could send out the first press release announcing the formation of her own agency the calls started coming in. Two years later she still thought about running a small publicity campaign for herself but also admitted that she never had the time to prepare it. Two nurses who opened a private storefront practice in a small Appalachian community did not even think about garnering publicity to announce themselves simply because they knew nothing about it. Fortunately for them, they did not need it. When they showed up for work that first Monday morning, the line of patients was twenty people deep. So before you place an ad, or, for that matter, go after any kind of publicity, consider how it will help.

Most marketing approaches will not work for most free-lancers. You probably cannot offer discounts, jazz up your service, dramatize the difference between you and your competition, or run a sale. The fact that most kinds of marketing will not work for you does not, however, mean that you cannot advertise and/or publicize. Consider it a blessing, however, that billboards, television, and radio not only are too expensive, but also usually wrong for your kind of business. Many free-lancers do have success with flyers, brochures, and small ads in trade journals and trade newspapers.

Planning an Advertising Program

However you decide to advertise, here are the steps you should follow:

1. Establish a budget. Decide how much—or how little—you can spend, and stick to it.

2. Investigate the media that are open to you—print, direct mail, posters, letters.

3. Establish a goal; that is, figure out exactly what you hope to accomplish by advertising. For free-lancers, this often means one of two things: You either want to remind old customers of your services, or you want to find new ones.

4. Set the timing of your program. Do not advertise during the busy seasons when you are swamped with work or during the holiday seasons when no one thinks about work. On the other hand, the ideal time to advertise is when you can see the end of a long, busy season or right after the holidays when everyone returns to work geared up to make up for the lost time.

The Value of Advertising

Keep in mind that advertising is not something you must do, and you certainly should not do it if you will not gain anything from it. Studies show that—and this must apply especially to free-lancers—print ads are less effective advertising tools than are personal communications. Since personal communication is the keystone of building a free-lance business, do not push yourself to advertise in any other way if you have a booming business without doing so.

Remember, too, that as a free-lancer, you may be your own best advertisement. You are always promoting yourself or your free-lance business, even when you may think of yourself as being off-duty. Whenever people congregate, the topic of work usually comes up—and free-lancers are often a subject of great interest to others. As you explain your services to others, you are often, even unknowingly, making a pitch for future business. And when you free-lance you are selling yourself every bit as much as your skills. Therefore it stands to reason that the personal touch is still the most effective, especially for free-lancers.

If you do decide to advertise, almost without exception the ads you use will be print ads. Few free-lancers can afford or need to use radio or television. Print ads may be done in black and white or color. Color is far more expensive than black and white. A black-and-white ad could include a photograph, and for many photographers, artists, and designers, this is the best way to show off work, although free-lancers who do not work in the arts can use a simple typographical ad, that is, an ad composed entirely of words as opposed to photographs or drawings.

If you work in a related field, you will already know how to go about producing your own ads or where to find someone to help you create them. If you have never done anything like this, the best thing to do is to turn to someone who does know how to create an ad—either a commercial artist or a designer. Look for someone who free-lances because he or she will probably be more sympathetic to your needs. No matter how small your ad or how friendly you are with the person, you should not expect someone to do this work for you for free, although you might see if you can swap some of your services for the ad you need.

Once the ad has been designed and put in final format, it is ready to go to a printer. Printers' work ranges from very expensive to fairly cheap, and the quality also ranges from excellent to poor. For your purposes you probably need a printer who does good-enough work for relatively little money. They do exist. Printers in that category are often called instant printers. They are one- or two-person businesses, often located in storefronts, that specialize in fast service. They print in quantity—200 or 500 may be their minimum.

Before you give your ad to a printer, ask to see some samples of his work and ask to see the price list. Check the samples to be sure the type or artwork is straight and well positioned on the page, and be sure the type is legible—it should not be blurred or too lightly or too heavily printed. If the quality of the printer's work suits you, leave your ad with him. Instant printers also have a fairly limited supply of papers; if you want anything unusual, you will have to buy it from an art or business supply store.

When you pick up your work, be sure to look at it while you are still at the printer's shop. If you do not like what you see (the type runs down the page instead of across or the o's are filled with ink), then complain right away. The printer will usually do the job over at no extra cost to you, provided the error is his. On the other hand, if you ordered brown ink and you now think it looks horrible, that is your problem and you will have to pay for reprinting.

Occasionally, an enterprising free-lancer decides to advertise by some unusual means. One free-lance landscaper sent special calendars to his clients each January. The calendars were designed with gardeners in mind and were a good reminder to his clients that the time to use his services was drawing near. A free-lance publicist sent ballpoint pens printed with her name and phone number to a number of clients as Christmas gifts. If you decide you want to do something like this, check the Yellow Pages for the names of companies that specialize in such items. And if you buy any office supplies in bulk by direct mail, you will soon be receiving catalogs advertising these promotion items.

While you may have fun buying and sending these self-promotion items (nothing is more tempting than these catalogues on a slow day), keep in mind that they may not be right for your business and could even hurt you more than they help you. If yours is a business where you rarely lunch with clients and Christmas gifts or even Christmas cards are unheard of, then steer clear of such gimmicks.

Free-lance Publicity

Publicity is a different matter from advertising in that you do not pay for publicity, whereas advertising is bought and sold. Stephanie Winston, who started her business as a personal organizer at a time when no one else had yet thought of doing such a thing professionally, had no choice but to go after publicity. Otherwise, no one would know she existed, and people would not understand what she did. Simply running an advertisement describing her personal organizing service was probably not going to work well since she was onto something new—about which the buying public had yet to be informed. Winston acknowledges that she went after the publicity she received by writing press releases that she sent to local New York City newspapers. Her efforts resulted in publicity from *The New York Times*, *The Village Voice*, and *The Wall Street Journal*.

Another woman, who developed a wardrobe consulting service, also focused on publicity as opposed to advertising as her best means of spreading the word about her free-lance business. She even acts as her own publicity agent, although she uses a different name when she sends press releases.

Among the devices through which an enterprising free-lancer can get publicity are write-ups in newspapers and magazines, appearances on television and radio shows, speeches to local groups, seminars and other forms of teaching, and attending meetings where potential customers congregate.

The amount and kind of publicity you get usually depends on whom you know. You can infiltrate your local media with press releases, and if your business is interesting or unusual enough, you will probably get some response. If lots of free-lancers do the work you do, though, you will not be a hot news item, and that's all there is to it.

With good contacts you can probably get yourself some small write-ups in the local paper or a spot appearance or a local radio or television show. Before you put much time and effort into setting this up, though, make sure you truly need it to get your business off the ground.

You can write the press releases and make the follow-up telephone calls yourself or you can hire a publicist—free-lance, if you like—or a publicity firm to do this for you. Hiring someone to do publicity is very expensive, though, and there are no promises of results, so most free-lancers operating on a shoestring are advised to make their own publicity contacts.

Advertising in Journals and Directories

Although not advertising in the strictest sense of the word, you should always take advantage of any opportunity to list yourself in a directory. Even if you do have to pay, the fee is usually relatively small compared to what a quarter or half-page advertisement would cost in some other place.

When you do advertise or list yourself in a directory, try to play up something about you that is different. One enterprising literary agent began his business by promoting himself as the agent who could deliver any kind of writer an editor needed. Editors soon came to him for the steady kind of backlist books that were not especially exciting and often were not blockbusters, but which brought in steady royalties over several years. Eventually, he sold the blockbuster books, too, but he was smart enough to start out by setting himself apart from the pack. If you are willing to do rush work or work over weekends, play that up. If your rates are cheaper than the going rates, that is also a strong advertising feature.

Keep in mind, though, that free-lance advertising is generally low-key, so do not spend much time and money preparing an advertising campaign that is not necessary—and more important, that will not bring you a substantially larger chunk of business.

Mailing Lists—How to Use Them

Apart from advertisements and listings in professional journals and directories, free-lancers in many areas report using a mailing list to advertise their services. One reason that this is especially useful for free-lancers is that you already have the base needed to establish your own mailing list. As you build contacts you are also building a potential mailing list—and there is no reason not to cash in on it. Barbara Zimmerman, who has used a mailing list with great success, reports, "It's been fascinating. I mail not to the people I work for, but to the people I don't work for. I started out with a general mailing list to my regular customers, but I quit. They will call me anyway, if they need me. I now mail twice a year. I always get five phone calls from the mailing list, which includes maybe several hundred names.

"I do a flyer. I cull the list carefully, too. I've discovered an agent market for my copyright services, so they get one mailing. My list is personal. I like to find the person with the need and authority to hire me. That's why I need a highly specialized list."

The first thing to keep in mind when planning to use a mailing list is that the basic list itself must be large because the response will be small. Direct mail experts expect a response rate of under 5 percent when they mail to potential customers, so you will need a list of several hundred to get five to ten calls. And the calls are just the beginning; fewer of those persons will actually become money-paying customers.

The kind of mailing you do depends upon the service you offer. The easiest mailing is a one-page flyer touting your services. A sample flyer sent by one free-lancer follows. Alternately, you might be better off sending a personal letter describing your services. Artists and photographers, as well as commercial artists and designers, often send flyers that include reproductions of their work.

As for the elbow grease required to prepare the mailing, this is something you can do at home with little effort or you can hire it done by someone with a machine that addresses and sorts labels. Such services are inexpensive, and if your list is over two hundred names, they may be worth paying. If your mailing list is under two hundred names, you may find it easier and cheaper to address the flyers or letters yourself.

Keep the mailing list personal. There are services that sell names and addresses, and you can also go to a trade directory of your particular field (and you may even need to do this if you are just starting out), but as soon as possible develop your own mailing list. This is an important key to establishing a high-response list.

P E R M I S S I O N S

Do you have a problem in the rights and permissions area that you would like a knowledgable negotiator to handle? My service is unique in offering this expertise on a freelance basis. My service clears permissions for the communications industry-books, filmstrips, records. You can call upon it for everything from obtaining the right to use art on a book or record cover to clearing an entire book, or a single permission, to obtaining a music license or the rush reading of a manuscript to determine what has to be cleared. Need some general advice about what's public domain material or what's fair use? Like someone to figure out what permissions you need for the second edition of a book? My service can solve all these problems for you.

OTHER SPECIALIZED SERVICES

1. <u>Copyright registration and renewal</u> - my service will do either or both on a freelance basis. A reminder that all works copyright between January 1, 1953 and December 31, 1977 must be renewed or they will fall into the public domain. 1981 is the year for renewing all material originally copyrighted in 1953.

2. <u>Granting permissions</u> on behalf of authors, small agencies and publishing houses.

3. <u>Estimating the costs of anthologies in advance</u> - all you have to do is send along your projected table of contents to get a realistic idea of fees, find out if royalties are involved and pinpoint any problem areas.

4. <u>Following up on permission payments</u> - you might be surprised at the fees you'd collect if you hired my service to follow up on permissions you've granted and request payment or a statement that the material has not been reprinted.

5. <u>Providing addresses</u> for people and firms that are hard-to-locate.

Whatever your problem may be in the rights and permissions area -
my service can solve it for you.

Using a Portfolio

In commercial and fine arts fields, portfolios are used as advertisements. Arranging your portfolio is a serious and time-consuming task—and surprisingly, one that you may not be best suited for. Certainly, you should get several opinions from friends before deciding on a final shape for your portfolio, and if you have an agent or representative, his opinion should also be taken into consideration. Some representatives insist on arranging the portfolios themselves, although this occurs mostly on a commercial level. If your agent wants the right to arrange your portfolio, by all means agree; you want the person to sell your work, and he or she will do that best if he has had some control over the presentation of the work.

IF YOUR MARKETING PLAN WORKS

You will know your marketing plan has begun to work for you when repeat work comes in. If your plan has been very successful, the work may even pour in, possibly in a volume that you are not prepared to cope with. One happy free-lancer, the recipient of free publicity bestowed by a major newspaper article, answered her phone starting at 9:00 A.M. on the day the article ran and did not stop answering until 9:00 P.M. that night, after taking over one hundred calls. She had more business than she could handle if only 10 percent of the calls turned into jobs. Should you be this lucky, you will also have to be prepared to handle the flow of work, and this usually means that you will have to subcontract and possibly expand your equipment.

On the other hand, if you know for sure that you never want to do either of these things, then be sure to keep your marketing efforts low-key and aim them toward maintaining your present clientele once you have reached the number of clients you need to support yourself.

Subcontracting

For a free-lancer's purposes, subcontracting occurs when you hire someone to do the work you cannot handle or when you hire someone to handle those aspects of your work that you no longer have time for or do not want to handle. When business booms, for example, a free-lance business consultant might hire another consultant, a copywriter, or secretarial help. There are several ways you will know when it is time to subcontract:

- Is business seasonal? Are you so busy at some times of the year that you can barely manage a good night's sleep? Rather than turning away business, think about subcontracting.

- Is a lot of overtime required to complete your assignments or jobs?

- Could you spread your peak work times throughout the year, perhaps by juggling deadlines or putting clients on hold for several weeks or months, or is the work flow something you are unable to control or regulate? If the latter is true, you need to subcontract during the peak periods.

- Do you often miss deadlines or ask for extensions? Nothing may be wrong except that you have too much work. It is time to get help.

- How much in advance can you schedule your work? Are lots of jobs rush ones? If you answer "well in advance" and "yes," then you are a candidate for subcontracting.

There are several ways to subcontract. You can hire temporary help. You can hire a colleague who works for you directly on specific projects and receives a salary from you. You can send work out to a colleague or clerical service and take a cut of the pay. The job still goes through you, and you submit the bill and pay the subcontractee, but you lose some control over the quality of the work when you do this.

Temporary Help

Temporary help is an excellent time-saver, and since time is money, although you pay for these services, they are generally worth every penny. There are advantages and disadvantages to hiring temporary office help. Temporary office help works especially well when:

- You cannot afford to put someone on the payroll.

- The workload is uneven.

- You do not want to have to keep records on a full- or even part-time employee.

- Workers are available on short notice.

- You do not want to bother with training or interviewing employees.

Temporary help does not work well when:

- Too much time will be required to break someone in.

- You work in a small home office and dislike having someone in your home or feel you cannot work well alongside someone.

- A temporary worker may not be able to handle the variety of tasks that are routine for most free-lancers.

There are several ways to find good temporary help, word-of-mouth being among the best. Ask other business owners and clients who may use temporary help. The Yellow Pages or help wanted ads in a trade journal will usually reveal several agencies that specialize in temporary help. If you do deal with an agency, discuss the services they offer and explain exactly what your needs are. Ask about bonding and insurance, especially if the worker will be coming to your home. Temporary workers are paid by the hour.

Before a temporary worker or, for that matter, any kind of worker comes to your home, there are several things to do to prepare for him or her:

1. First estimate your needs to determine what kind of worker you want to hire. Don't get someone with higher or lower qualifications than you need.

2. Plan the kind of work that needs to be done.

3. Find a place for the person to do the work.

4. Plan the workload, that is, decide how much time you think should be allotted for specific projects. You still must allow the worker the freedom to work at an individual pace, but some guidance from you is wise.

5. Decide how much supervision you will offer. This is important to convey to the agency or person you hire; some people work well as self-starters; others dislike working this way and will not want to take a job where this is required.

6. Even though you plan to discuss the work with the person, also leave written directions regarding the work and where things are.

7. When the temporary worker arrives, show him or her to the place where the work is to be done and explain the work briefly.

Using temporary workers in a free-lance business probably calls for some lowering of your expectations. If you get a jewel who immediately understands the nature of your work, who is comfortable working in your home, and who does not mind working very hard, then you have hit a streak of luck. You are more likely to end up with someone who does not understand your work, does not want to work very hard, and who is slightly uncomfortable with your home office and (usually) old equipment. If the person works satisfactorily, then overlook these things. On the other hand, if you do not like the person or feel that he or she is incapable of doing the work, then report this immediately to the agency. You should not have to pay if you make this known right away. If you have hired the person on your own, you should still say something as soon as you realize the arrangement will not work. Pay the person for whatever time he or she has put in, and dismiss him or her politely but firmly.

Subcontracting work to a colleague can be either easier or harder than hiring a temporary worker, depending upon your point of view and the kind of work you want done. Keep in mind that often you are subcontracting work that you really do not want to do, and this will not make your colleague any happier than it makes you. On the other hand, the advantage of using a colleague is that you will be working with an equal, someone who is fully qualified to handle the work.

Subcontracting agreements vary depending upon the kind of work involved and the personal and professional relationship of the persons involved. Some free-lancers hire colleagues to handle their overflow and pay them slightly less than what they are earning for the job. A free-lance personal shopper earning $80 an hour might subcontract to a colleague for $50 an hour. Occasionally, a free-lancer subcontracts and pays the person who takes the work full price but still handles the billing and personal contact with the client. Obviously, there is no financial gain in doing this, but if you do not want to turn down a solid client, this may be a solution.

Leasing—The New-Equipment Solution

For some free-lancers, a surge of business also raises the question of buying more or better equipment. Since such surges may be seasonal or the result of advertising, though, it may be smarter to rent equipment rather than buying it—at least until you are sure that the new level of business is permanent. Leasing equipment is cheaper than buying it, and it often gives you a few months of breathing room until you decide whether or not you are going to make a go of something.

When you lease equipment, negotiate the agreement just as you would any other agreement. Here are some of the more common terms of leasing agreements:

- Do not pay a security deposit. The owner still owns his equipment, and he is protected if you default on payment.

- Do not accept an agreement that forces you to buy supplies or services from the lessor.

- Along the same line, do not accept an agreement that contains an unconditional guarantee to pay. Again, the person or company that rents you the equipment can always repossess, if necessary.

- Insist on a clause guaranteeing service in the contract, but do not buy a service contract. Service contracts are expensive, and you pay for service you may not need. If someone leases you equipment, he should be prepared to maintain it.

- Do not accept any escalator clauses except possibly on service—and you should fight that. Once you have a piece of equipment in your possession, its cost cannot go up; therefore, it is silly for you to pay more later than you did at the beginning of the contract. The cost of providing service may go up, but if you can strike a hard enough bargain, you should not have to pay for it during the course of one contract.

Too many free-lancers do less well than they should or find themselves faced with a sudden drop in business for the very simple reason that they have not planned for the future. They have not sought out new markets and new clients, nor have they maintained regular contact with their steady clients. Doing all these things involves setting up and following through on a marketing program, such as it may be in the free-lance world. Free-lancers need not do anything fancy along these lines, nor should a marketing program take much time or money, but you will not be successful if you expect to drift along without ever taking any actions to build or renew your business. There is a saying that a smart person starts looking for his next job the day he begins a new one. This is certainly true for anyone running a free-lance business. The day you settle down with lots of work, the day when you have developed a reliable roster of clients, is the very day that you should start rounding up new ones.

Measuring
Your Success

11

Let's face facts: Free-lancing is a glamorous business, at least to those outside the business looking in, and often, even to those who choose to free-lance. In addition to the glamour attached to free-lancing itself, many free-lancers work in the creative professions such as theater, the arts, or publishing. Another part of the appeal of free-lancing is the opportunity it provides to control not only your personal life but also your professional life. Unfortunately, because of the glamour attached to free-lancing, many free-lancers take a die-hard view of their chosen profession. They refuse to recognize the signs that it may be time to bail out. Although you may find it strange to find a discussion about the possibility of giving up in a chapter about success, at several points in a free-lance career giving up becomes an issue. Even highly successful free-lancers have to face the fact that this career may not be for them forever. The best way to consider whether or not it may be time for you to get out is to measure your success as a free-lancer.

MONEY AS A YARDSTICK OF
FREE-LANCE SUCCESS

If you think of free-lancing as a business and if you are goal-oriented in terms of your free-lance career, then money is one very big measure of your success. In most businesses, money is the only measure of success: If you are making a profit, then you are successful.

Success in free-lancing is more complex. Although money should definitely be one measure of your success, because of the unusual nature of free-lance work it is not the only one. For example, if you decided to free-lance because you wanted to write a book and had found that you could not find the time to do so any other way except by supporting yourself part-time as a free-lancer, then one measure of success for you would be: Did you find the time and discipline to write the book? Money becomes secondary. If you did make the time and money to write, then you were successful in your free-lancing venture. Underlying such issues, though, is the question of financial success. Ultimately it won't have done you any good to have found the time and discipline to write the book if you didn't earn enough money to live on while you wrote. Like it or not, money is the measure of success for a free-lancer even if the amount that means success varies greatly from person to person.

Determining whether or not you are a successful free-lancer is not so vague a matter as it might seem. For example, you can count yourself as successful if:

- You earn enough to satisfy you right now and can project that you will earn enough to satisfy you in the future.

- You view free-lancing as a full-time, long-term work. It may not last forever, but you aren't sending out ten resumes every Monday morning, either.

- You are truly enjoying your independence and freedom.

- You are not constantly worried about getting enough work or earning enough to maintain yourself in the style in which you like to be maintained. This does not mean you should not tolerate a few slow months or even a slow year, or that your business will not have its ups and downs, but overall you should be earning enough to live well according to your personal standards.

THINKING ABOUT BAILING OUT

If you cannot positively answer the list you just read, then you may have to consider the possibility that free-lancing is not the best career choice for you at the moment. It is important to keep in mind that there are legitimate reasons—some of them beyond your control—that may cause you to want to get out of free-lancing. You may be caught in a bad economy, and that is certainly beyond your control. If car manufacturers can have a bad year, or for that matter, a bad decade, then you can certainly see that a rotten economy can take its toll on one free-lancer—even one who is giving the business his or her best efforts.

Some people cannot free-lance because they lack the personality or temperament. Sometimes this just cannot be predicted in advance. You have to free-lance to find out it is not for you. One former free-lancer, now a happily employed managing editor with a major publisher, thought he had everything he needed to free-lance: lots of ambition, an ability to tolerate a considerable amount of time alone, a love of independence. Plus, he hated his job. Offered the chance to free-lance full-time, he quit his job the same day, bought some paper and pens, and considered himself in business. He recalled, "Within three months, I knew this wasn't for me. I missed the camaraderie of the office, the excitement of getting up and going to work every day. All the self-discipline I had when I worked for someone else—I always stayed late and took work home—just fell apart when I had to face whole days alone in my apartment. I got a full-time job with the company I was supposed to free-lance for as soon as one opened up."

Another former free-lancer wanted time off from the responsibilities of a full-time job to write a historical novel. She had done preliminary work on the book, including eliciting some interest from publishers. She considered herself in the writing business once she had resigned her full-time job, accepted a part-time job two days a week, and lined up three major free-lance projects over the coming year. She would have several months in which to do nothing but write her book, and this would be punctuated by several spates of free-lance work. It seemed like a writer's dream. Not only would she earn enough to live on with the free-lance projects and temporary work, but also she had set herself up with some time off from her writing so she could develop the necessary detachment to evaluate her work. What she didn't count on was her penchant for daydreaming. The same part of her personality that could conceive of an elaborate historical novel also kept her occupied for too many hours a day staring into space or out the window. She daydreamed about what her life would be like when she was a best-selling author. She daydreamed about returning to full-time work. She day-dreamed about how she would write her book. But she never actually wrote enough of it to show a publisher. Since her full-time work as a senior editor for a trade publisher had always kept her too busy for her thoughts to wander, she had not realized this would be a problem until she started free-lancing. Another unpredictable factor contributed to the demise of yet another free-lance career.

The third reason beyond your control that may cause you to get out of free-lancing is rapid technological change—the kind that is too much for you to keep up with. You either do not understand the technology, or you cannot afford to buy or up-date equipment. This happened to one free-lance typesetter, who reported, "I spent over $2,000 on a very fancy typewriter when I began to free-lance. I considered that a major invest-ment for me and took out a bank loan to pay for it. Suddenly, I needed a word processor for the kind of work I was doing. Had I known that from the beginning, I could have purchased it, but I could not add the debt of buying a word processor to the payments for my $2,000 typewriter. So I'm temporarily out of the free-lance business. I say temporarily because I'm plan-ning to buy a word processor as soon as I can afford one. I'm slowed down in my drive to work for myself, but not stopped."

Temporary or Permanent Bailout?

Most free-lancers recognize the signs that it is time to quit; they just don't want to give up on the dream. You can feel the restlessness, the ennui, the inability to discipline yourself growing. Signs that it is time to think about getting out include the following:

- You can barely pay the bills month after month.

- Instead of getting up early and eagerly tackling your work, you sleep later and later, take longer and longer lunches, and in short, just do not get much done during the day.

- You are bored and feel unchallenged.

- You are lonely, not for a few minutes, but most of the time.

- You are depressed.

- You are plagued with anxiety, which many persons use to ward off depression.

- You cannot expand your business enough to feel secure should you lose a major client.

- You cannot earn enough to take vacations. Anyone starting a business may skip vacations for a year or two, but if you have gone for years without a vacation, something is wrong.

- You cannot earn enough to put aside money for retirement.

If most of this list sounds rather alarmingly like your life, then you are in trouble as a free-lancer. Remember, though, that all work is cyclical. Everyone goes through ups and downs, good periods and bad. Be careful not to mistake temporary burnout for burnout that cannot be cured.

Another important way to tell whether you need to find yourself another career is to consider your motives for free-lancing. Why do you do it? For the glamour? The free time? The independence? These are not good enough reasons alone to keep you in the business: The work is simply too hard for that. Furthermore, consider that if you have a need to shine in front of people, a need that has kept you struggling to be an actor for fifteen years with little success, then you will probably apply that need to shine to whatever work you do. Which means you can shine at some other kind of job. Never mistake a love of glamour or a need to have a certain kind of attention for a love of the kind of work you do.

You should also reconsider when all your friends are making a lot more money than you are. There is nothing wrong with struggling at a career for a number of years—free-lancers and nonfree-lancers do that—but when everyone else seems to have pulled way out in front of you, that is another sign that it may be time to pull out.

Finally, if you constantly feel stressed or anxious, think about giving it up. The toll anxiety and stress take on your health is not worth it.

Once you contemplate getting out, consider whether this is likely to be a permanent or a temporary move. As one free-lancer noted, "I think I'm getting a little bored now, and I might look around for something else to do. But I know that I will free-lance at various points throughout my life. Perhaps I have not found the area to free-lance in. The idea of free-lancing has appeal to me, and I've done well at one free-lance business. I'm just not sure it is the right business." This feeling was echoed by many free-lancers. Just as there are personalities incapable of free-lancing, there are also persons who have a free-lance mentality in the very best sense of the word. Sometimes, these people only need a few years to find the right free-lance trade.

If you think you are leaving free-lancing temporarily because of a bad economy or while you look for another area in which to reestablish yourself, then you should take this into account when you wind down your free-lance business.

Making a Successful Exit from a Free-lance Business

Whether you are leaving free-lancing temporarily or perma-nently, there is an art to getting out gracefully.

If you are leaving temporarily, take care not to burn any bridges with your clients. One possibility is to turn your clients over to a colleague, but the disadvantage to doing this is that you may lose your clients permanently to another free-lancer. But if this is necessary to ensure good will between you and your clients and to smooth the path for the day when you may return to free-lancing, then it may be worth it.

If you decide not to supply your clients with another source of free-lance help, you should still notify them of your plans to leave the free-lancing business. And you should save all your files and contacts for a return engagement in the free-lance business.

It is almost impossible to sell a free-lance business, especially a one-person operation. You simply cannot promise someone that he or she will achieve the same volume of business you have, and since the business is based entirely on your ability to sell your services, there is not much else to sell. You could try to sell your contact file, but a smart free-lancer will know that the file is accessible for free in other places— such as the public library—or through the application of some elbow grease.

Many people panic at the thought of leaving free-lancing. However insecure and unhappy they may have felt as free-lancers, they are even more insecure and unhappy at the thought of returning to the world of working for someone else. Fears center around a number of issues. Will time spent free-lancing be lost time that can never be made up in your career? Will you have to take a job at a lower level than the job you held when you started free-lancing? Will you earn less money? What should you tell people you have been doing for the past few years? More important, will they believe you?

Keep this in mind: People will take you just as seriously as a free-lancer as you take yourself. If you paint a picture of someone who worked a four-hour day, often worked for starvation wages, and who had too much free time, then your free-lance efforts will not count for much when you start job hunting. On the other hand, if you paint a picture of yourself as someone capable of running a small business, someone with executive and administrative skills, someone able to sell himself or herself, then you will look very good indeed to a prospective employer.

There are two things to keep in mind as you exit gracefully from your free-lance life. First, play up your free-lance experience. Do it on a résumé and during interviews. Assume that you will be given credit not only for free-lancing but also for having run your own business.

Wind down slowly. Don't expect to find a job right away, especially if you want a job that is a vertical move from your last full-time job working for someone else. Finding the right job always takes time. And unlike someone who suddenly finds himself out of work unexpectedly and doesn't know how he will get by, you have already proved to yourself that you have the skill and acumen to earn a good living until you find the right job.

If You Decide to Continue Free-lancing

If all signs point toward the fact that yours is a successful free-lance business, then you probably don't need much advice. A few words will suffice:

- Keep a fairly tight rein on your financial status. Small business operators walk a tightrope between operating in the red and the black. You may always have to watch your financial status carefully.

- Always be on the lookout for new work and new assignments. Remember that there is no better time to look for more work than when you are very busy with your present work. Don't count on the same clients using you over and over again; instead, always keep a lookout for new possibilities.

- Always plan ahead, both for finding new work and new areas in which to work, and for investing in your future. If you don't handle this, no one else will.

- Always leave a little time for meditation and for seeking new directions. Free-lancing is the most flexible career path you can follow; just be sure that you maintain enough personal flexibility to always be ready for what lies ahead.

- The last word: Make sure you are enjoying yourself; otherwise, the creative endeavors, the long hours, the times when money is tight will not be worthwhile in the long run.

Index